PROMISE

Over

PURPOSE

Promise Over Purpose is a profound guide that shifts our focus from the relentless search for purpose to the sustaining power of God's promises. It's filled with wisdom and biblical truths that provide hope and direction in life's most challenging moments. Every page is a testament to the transformative power of living in God's promises. This is a must-read!

—Alli Worthington, Author and Business Coach

Over the years, I've sat with more than one woman as she agonized over not knowing her purpose in life. How would she know which direction to work and serve if she didn't know what God wanted her to do with her life? Danita bravely suggests a better path, gently encouraging her readers to consider that we've been looking at this from a too limited perspective, one that colors it with the wrong pressures. In this thought-provoking work, she challenged me to think more simply—and more broadly—toward the heart of God, who wants to do more in me and through me than I can ask or imagine. I walked away, encouraged by the billions of ways I can fulfill my God-given purpose today and every day hereafter.

—Carrie Daws, author of *The Warrior's Bride* and *Living in the Shadow of Death*

PROMISE

Over

PURPOSE

Unveiling the Path to a Peace-Filled Life

DANITA CUMMINS

Promise over Purpose

Copyright© 2024 by Danita Cummins

Library of Congress Cataloging-in-Publication Data

LCCN: 2024915179 (paperback) ISBN: 978-1-961732-25-4 (ebook) | ISBN: 978-1-961732-24-7 (paperback) | ISBN: 978-1-961732-26-1 (audiobook)

Published in association with Called Creatives Publishing, www.calledcreativespublishing.com

Cover design: Steve Kuhn

Interior design: Dallas Hodge

2024 – First Edition

DEDICATION

To Liz,
I hope I answered your questions.

To April,
I hope heaven is better than we imagined it could be.

TABLE OF CONTENTS

Introduction   5

Part I: The Purpose Paradox   18

  Chapter 1: Our Quest for Purpose   19

  Chapter 2: The Anxiety of Purpose   37

  Chapter 3: God's Perfect Plan   53

  Chapter 4: The Promises of God   69

  Reflection: Unwrapping Your Purpose Paradox   83

Part II: The Idol of Purpose   90

  Chapter 5: Rediscovering Your Identity in Christ   91

  Chapter 6: When Purpose Becomes Performance   108

  Chapter 7: The Sanctity of Suffering   131

  Chapter 8: The Freedom to Surrender   148

  Reflection: Releasing the Idol of Purpose   164

Part III: Living in the Promise   172

  Chapter 9: Embracing a Life of Promise   173

  Chapter 10: Choosing the Confidence of Grace   191

  Chapter 11: Seeking the Clarity of Wisdom   208

  Chapter 12: Trusting in God's Provision   223

  Chapter 13: A Billion Different Ways   238

  Reflection: Practicing Promise Over Purpose   256

Afterword   263

Acknowledgments   268

Endnotes   272

FOREWORD

When I encounter a serious new book, I consider its credibility. For me, credibility is made up of two parts: The author and the content. I read and carefully considered the author and the content of this book, *Promise Over Purpose: Unveiling the Path to a Peace-filled Life*. I found both to be sound and reliable. I give *Promise Over Purpose* my strongest recommendation. If you read only one book in this present season of your life, it should be this one.

The author of the book you are holding is Danita Cummins. She is a wordsmith—She calls herself a worder. Danita has a proven ability to find just the right words, and just the right story to express her point. Danita fills many roles. In her own words, she wears many hats, including, "mom, wife, Christian, military spouse, daughter, sister, writer, founder, and podcaster." She is also kind, wise, and an effective communicator. She is a nice person with a nice sense of humor. She is a respected business professional. She effectively leads a nonprofit in Fayetteville, North Carolina, Danita has deep experience in leading professionals and organizations in strategic planning exercises. I know because she led such efforts at the nonprofit I led for several years, as well as at the church where I serve. Danita is a seeker. She asks good questions—the kind of questions that most thoughtful people are also asking. Danita is full of love; if you have the privilege of spending time with her, you will find that she is also full of grace—for all people. Danita sincerely believes people are doing the best they can and she regularly helps brothers and sisters on their journey. Finally, Danita is a person of deep Christian faith. She is a child of God. She is close to Jesus. Danita has the proven ability to draw other people closer to Jesus. If you carefully read her book, you will deepen your own faith, and you will find yourself closer to Jesus, too.

From Danita, I've relearned the difference between roles and identity. I fill multiple roles, too. I am a father, husband, military veteran, business professional, sincere friend, and pastor. I am a Christian; I am a Jesus-follower. Most of these are roles, they are not my deepest identity. They are not my purpose. Think about your identity; release it, if necessary. Most importantly, I am a contributing family member; I am a person who helps people; I am a servant leader; and I am an encourager. More than anything, I am a child of God too.

The content of *Promise Over Purpose* is solid. This content reminds me of my years as a cadet at a military college. I was soaked in the concepts of Duty, Honor, and Country—But mostly Duty. "Always do your nearest duty."[1] Such instruction is valuable because it can fill you with purpose—For a time. And then what? Certainly, a sense of purpose is good, but what about when the pursuit of purpose gets out of balance? Can you make an idol of something good like purpose? Yes. Danita says such an imbalance in your life leads to loneliness, discouragement, and anxiety. Danita points to a better focus—on God's purposes and God's promises. God wants you to get to know Him and enjoy Him; to live into His purposes for you; to serve and to love; and to witness to God's goodness.

Danita addresses pitfalls on this journey, such as Cultural Conformance, Control, Comparison, and, again, making an idol of Purpose. And she calls us to shift our focus, to find our identity in Jesus Christ alone.

Danita promises that peace is possible. And aren't we all looking for deep, inner peace? So many of the stories in the Bible point to this yearning for peace. The Children of Israel longed for a place of peace, when they fled hundreds of years of slavery in Egypt (Exodus 12). God's people again longed for peace and protection, from the fearsome Philistines, when David had his epic face-to-face fight against Goliath (as recorded in 1 Samuel 17). When Jesus meets the Samaritan Woman at the Well, in John 4, she has a restless soul, and is thirsty for Jesus' kind of peace. In Mark 4, Jesus' disciples find themselves in the middle of a terrible storm, and they cry out to Jesus to stop it. In Verse 39, Jesus orders the storm to be still; declares peace; and the winds quiet down, and all is still. During His earthly ministry, Jesus goes around preaching, teaching, and healing—and proclaiming peace and freedom and rest. In John 14:27, Jesus says, "Peace I leave with you; my peace I give you. I do not give to you as the world gives. Do not let your hearts be troubled and do not be afraid." Finally, Saint Paul the Apostle tells us, in Romans 5:1, that when you and I place our full faith and trust in Jesus, we have peace with God through Jesus. That's Good News. Today is your day. If you allow it, the Holy Spirit is with you and in you, and leading you (and me) into such a place of peace.

Again, Danita asks good questions. She asks, "What would your life be like if you focused on Gods' promises instead of chasing after purpose?" And, "How can you live a life where all of God lives through all of you?" These are good questions.

Danita points to God's purpose in our lives as (Jesus speaking), *"Love the Lord your God with all your heart and with all your soul and with all your mind and with all your strength. The second is this: 'Love your neighbor as yourself.'"* (Mark 12:30-31). Christians embrace this Jesus-teaching as the Great Commandment. ...

Commit to God, to help you live this out. Love God; Love people; and so, change the world.

Danita defines God's promises as, "...obligations that He imposes upon Himself." I find this definition to be helpful and encouraging. Danita states that there are more than 8,000 of God's promises in the Bible, at least 8,810 of them. Danita provides a list of some of them, with the source chapter and verse.

Danita talks about God's amazing grace in your life. She includes Six Simple Steps to focus on God's Amazing Grace, every day. She points out, accurately, that your life is not about work. It's about the saving grace of Jesus."

Danita created this book in an easy-to-read format and length. Again, she includes lots of supporting stories, analogies, and exercises. She concludes every chapter with a short prayer—to help you find just the right words—to reconnect with God.

Ultimately, Danita writes about placing your full faith and trust in a good God. Every moment of every ordinary day. This is a meaningful book. I hope you enjoy it as much as I did. When you read it carefully, through the eyes of faith, it will change your life—for the better.

Blessings,

Marv Gordner

Pastor, Black's Chapel Methodist Church

INTRODUCTION

Promise Over Purpose

"I don't know my purpose," admitted the beautiful girl, uncertainty looming in her soft brown eyes. Each Sunday evening, as youth group leaders, my husband and I explored life's challenges and questions with teenagers as we sat in plastic chairs in the makeshift classrooms at church.

Eventually, this week's topic moved to purpose. I looked around the room at the ambitious students and watched their expressions mirror hers. As I studied her face, I felt the weight of her confession. It was as if she were admitting to her faults or failures because she hadn't yet found her purpose. But that confession implied a deeper question: *"What is wrong with me?"*

I contemplated how she could carry the weight of that statement at 15. She's just beginning to lean into herself, to find her voice and discover her hidden heart.

So, why, at this moment, does she feel the weight or anxiety of trying to find her purpose? What is causing her to seek out the answer to a seemingly unanswerable question?

At first, the thought of her carrying this responsibility was incredulous and unnecessary. But as I looked across the table, I saw how the other girls seemed to carry it as well. They nodded in silent defeat as if to say, "Yeah, me too. I don't know my purpose either."

My heart ached for their despair. Couldn't they see themselves as I did, beautiful and loved beyond measure?

Didn't they know they were held by a loving Savior who promised to walk with them through every step and moment of their life?

Couldn't they see a future filled with endless possibilities and hope?

At that moment, the answer seemed to be "No."

I leaned forward and offered a small piece of encouragement. "Purpose is not something you do or wear. It's not something that God issues to you when you're born," I said. "Purpose is more about your unique design; it will look different in each season of your life." I paused as the girl gazed at me from across the table.

"God has called us to two things," I told them. "First, to love Him with your entire heart, soul, mind, and strength. Second, to love your neighbor as yourself. The first is almost impossible and, if we're honest, will take us a lifetime to achieve. The second can be done in a billion different ways."

I watched my words settle like dust, leaving nothing but vacant spaces in its path. Moments passed as they considered their truth, but they offered no reply.

"So, don't carry the weight of it," I pleaded. "God doesn't intend for you to carry this burden."

I felt the urgency of that message deep within my spirit. But in my heart, I recognized their doubt as my own.

We sat silently, looking across the table as clouds of confusion hovered in the room. After a few rounds of small talk, the session ended. As we departed into the crisp fall evening, I carried home more questions than answers.

Contemplating the Questions

Over several weeks, I contemplated our conversation. Their words played over and over like a soundtrack stuck on repeat. As I looked at the question, I considered their confessions. I prayed and asked the Lord to lift the weight of the pressure they seemed to carry. But as I pondered their question, new ones appeared.

I asked the Lord:

- What *is* our purpose, exactly?
- Where does our *purpose* come from?
- Can it be found?
- Have you given each of us one special gift, placed deep within our unique design, that only we can see?
- Is "What is my purpose?" the wrong question to ask?

Over the next few months, I discovered a radically different perspective, realizing our fixation on purpose needs to change. Chasing after purpose, like it is a prize to capture, isn't the point! God's holy power and sovereign provision undergird our Christian lives. They are earmarked with a promise of everlasting love.

If we spend our lives chasing after purpose, our lives are filled with confusion and doubt.

At times, purpose seems ambiguous and causes degrees of anxiety or fear. Conversely, God's promises are filled with immeasurable hope. They are eternal and life-sustaining.

What would life look like if we replaced our pursuit of purpose with relying on God's promises each day?

Before we go on, I know it seems like a simple question. And I acknowledge that living through God's promises is not a simple process. The journey to find purpose and meaning in our lives seems daunting. But I would offer you a different perspective. What if we shift our focus to a life of promise over purpose?

We must begin this journey by asking harder questions.

Asking Harder Questions

Do you like solving tricky problems like linear equations? For a small minority, the answer might be yes. But for most of us, it's a resounding "No." After attempting to answer the question on our own or recalling the specific formula needed, we pause and ask, "Is the answer in the back of the book?"

The back of the book is our safety net. When teachers handed out math books on the first day of class, I flipped to the back of the towering textbook to find the answers. They allowed math-tight-rope walkers like me to edge across the openness of an undiscovered landscape. We moved between the known and unknown as the ambiguous space enveloped us.

While math may not excite you, I'm sure you found great solace knowing the answers were there if you ever needed them.

But what happens if the answers aren't in the back of the book? What if you discover you're stuck after you've tried to solve the problem? You face the reality that you're lost and don't know where to go. The keywords or index of resources cannot point you in the right direction to find the next piece to solve your puzzle.

That's where I sat as I launched the quest to understand the Christian pursuit of purpose and to find the answers to this elusive mist. I struggled because there were no answers in the back of the book.

My book was blank.

This has been a discovery journey for me as I've tried to unpack these questions:

- What is the meaning and definition of purpose?
- What is the theology and psychology of it?
- Why are we inundated with it now in our culture and lives?
- Why does it cause such anxiety, shame, and guilt?
- Why do we, regardless of age or social standing, seem to need it, desire to find it, search for it, pray about it, and long to find the answer to a seemingly unanswerable question?
- If purpose causes anxiety and doubt, is there a better way to live?

That is what this book strives to define. But it's more than just a study about "purpose." It's a resource to help you release the weight and burden of trying to "find your purpose" like a lost treasure hidden from view. It offers God's promises in return.

The Hidden Purpose

The weight of asking, "What is my purpose?" and trying to find the answer seems daunting. If we're honest, it's unbearable at times. It leaves us with anxiety, guilt, and a lack of peace, which is not by God's holy design.

We ask, "What is our purpose? Where does it come from? Where does it go? How does it move, shape, and grow as the seasons of our life change? Is it a constant, one thing set inside us when our soul was created, or is it a function of our lives, constantly moving and changing?

And how do we respond when things like cancer, infant loss, or war seep into those spaces? How do we reconcile the pain of our life with our purpose?"

It's hard. It's really hard sometimes. I admit my own failures and fears as I tried, without success, to answer the question.

Over the years, I found myself defeated or frustrated, searching for the answer to this mystical question. But I continued to return to one fundamental truth: **God promises to love us forever.**

That is true. That is constant. That promise remains when everything else seems to be screaming at us to move, change, grow, strive, challenge, or give all of ourselves to our careers, vocations, families, churches, and the world.

So, if that one promise always remains true, are there others? Are there other promises we can cling to when our pursuit of purpose becomes too great to bear?

The answer is Yes. There are thousands of promises. But the only way to see them is to ask tougher questions. And we start with this one:

What promises can we see, hold, and curl up inside when purpose seems to fade away?

The answer: *All of them.*

To replace our pursuit of purpose with the promises of God, we must change the basis of our perspective, bolster our faith, and believe in His everlasting love. We do that when we decide to stop chasing after purpose.

Chasing Purpose

The more I see the world, specifically the church, chasing after purpose, the more it saddens my heart. The pursuit of purpose often brings anxiety and doubt. Our cultures and congregations, including those I love, grasp at purpose like a life raft. This clutching leads me to question if the pursuit of purpose is part of a greater deception.

- Is our pursuit of purpose an idol?
- If it isn't, have we been deceiving ourselves?
- If we haven't, why does it cause such anxiety, shame, and guilt?

I laid these questions before the Lord and found this simple yet complex answer:

"Our purpose is to allow <u>all of God</u> to live through <u>all of us</u>."

We are called to live a life that is <u>fully alive</u> in Christ. And that, dear friend, can be a daunting journey.

For Christians, our purpose is clear. We strive to create a life where **all of God lives through all of us.** We do that by acknowledging His divine purpose and allowing our identity to be rooted and established in His promises. We surrender to His love across our entire life, in both the good and the grievous moments.

His Divine Purpose

Our purpose is rooted within a deep well of scriptures and sovereignty. We find it first in the *Shema* and later in Jesus's teaching in the Gospel of Matthew.

We are called to do two things:

1) Love the Lord your God
2) Love your neighbor as yourself

But how we do that amid our thoughts, actions, beliefs, doubts, fears, and suffering varies. The ways are endless, a never-ending labyrinth of lanes to explore. And we struggle, at times, to see the guiding lampposts laid out before us. But God offers one simple truth to answer our purpose question: Love me and love the world.

One Simple Truth

At face value, it seems simple: to live a life where **all of God** lives through **all of me.**

But how do we do that? That is the hard part, friend. It's messy, confusing, and frustrating. But it's also passionate, peaceful, and filled with endless joy.

We search for a specific roadmap or a 5-step plan to "find our purpose," but I believe we're asking the wrong questions.

Discovering the path and steps we should take each day to live a life *fully alive* in Christ requires an entirely different perspective. When we try to imprison God's sovereignty into a five-point plan, we attempt to secure, in our futility, the magnitude and magnificence of a holy, divine, omnipresent, infinite God.

QUITE SIMPLY, GOD IS NOT A 5-STEP PLAN.

Quite simply, God is not a 5-step plan.

So, if the "What is my purpose?" question is wrong, what do we ask instead? How do we live amid the trials and tribulations of life and find peace in the in-between spaces between life and the everlasting?

Here's my offering to you!

Instead of asking, "What is my purpose?" ask these two things:

1) What can you cling to, hang your hat on, build your life around, and store in your hidden heart that will sustain you when the winds of life blow at your door?

2) What framework can you use to build your life and faith so that you have the peace of knowing that no matter what the world, the church, or your community says, you are living a life *fully alive* and inspired by divine purpose?

The answer: *God's promises.*

By knowing His promises, we find our purpose, which is simply to love God and the world. In that knowing, we answer our questions. Every answer is found in Christ alone.

- His sacrifice becomes our prosperity.
- His surrender becomes our protection.
- His salvation becomes our provision.
- His serenity becomes our peace.
- His sanctity becomes our purpose.

It's the ultimate paradox, which requires us to shift our perspective.

Shifting Your Perspective

Purpose seems to move like time. We can't hold it. It shifts around us, but we don't quite understand it. I liken it to dreams or the wind. Like the soul, we wonder what it is made of. Where does it come from, or where does it go?

These questions, like the making of the constellations, are complex. They have been asked many times across many generations. And so, I do not claim to be a great philosopher or social psychologist who can answer them. I only offer a different perspective, rooted in this one simple truth: God is a God of love—always. In His promises, we find the blessed assurance, as the old hymns say, that keeps us grounded. His promises allow us to take one more breath on dark days.

In them, we discover the Lord's newness and fresh love on frigid winter nights. We find the solid arms of a protective Savior as we lay curled on the bathroom floor, the sobs of our sorrows muffled into a worn and ragged rug.

And in those moments, there is purpose. It might look different from how we think it should look or feel. But in those moments, we are loved beyond compare. We have His promises. And we get a glimpse, for as much as our human frailty can stand, of the Father's heart this side of heaven.

When the answers to my purpose questions seem unclear, I return to this foundational promise: "I have loved you with an everlasting love,"[2] as the Scripture says.

That promise prompts me to ask alternative questions because in those answers, I find His love.

Asking Alternative Questions

Today, I offer you two new questions:

1) **What would your life be like if you focused on God's promises instead of chasing after purpose?**
2) **How can you live a life where *all of God* lives through *all of you*?**

Those are the questions I hope to help you answer.

Seeking our purpose without holding onto the promises of God is futile. The promises are like the secret decoder ring. Without them, there is no purpose. Without the promises, we have nothing but ourselves and our empty plight to fill the unquenchable thirst in our souls.

God's promises are not limited to those in this book. They are more significant and incredible than I could ever capture. But I pray this journey helps you, dear friend, replace your purpose anxiety with the promises of God so they can carry and sustain you on difficult days. Through that gift, you will develop the peace and joy of knowing that you are living fully in Him. And in that process, you will see how His promises remain. Those are the rocks we cling to. Those are the gifts we gather. He is our only hope. Our *purpose* rests in Him alone.

This book is designed in three parts, with reflection questions at the end of each section to help you unwrap your purpose questions. I've placed a prayer at the end of each chapter as an offering to allow God's love and wisdom to shine through your story.

Let's start with this prayer of encouragement for you:

A Prayer for the One Who Seeks to Discover Their Purpose

Dear Lord,

I pray that my dear friend, the one reading this book, will discover Your promises in new and powerful ways. As we walk through these chapters and stories together, may You offer gentle grace and bold courage, allowing them to see Your love and promises with life-changing faith. May our time together bring honor and glory to You above all else. May they always see Your face.

Amen.

PART I: THE PURPOSE PARADOX

OUR QUEST FOR PURPOSE

No man can tell another what [his] purpose is.
Each must find out for himself and
accept the responsibility that his answer prescribes.

—Dr. Victor Frankl, *Man's Search for Meaning*

I f you could have any superpower, what would it be? After being a mermaid, I'd settle on time travel. So, hop into my DeLorean time machine and travel with me back to 1984.

We're sitting in the 4th-grade classroom at Rose Witcher Elementary School. It's an average brick building at the end of an average suburban street. I fidget in the spare chair beside Mrs. Stanley's large wooden desk as my 10-year-old feet barely touch the tile floor. It's the seat reserved for children who need a little help. As the students linger in small groups behind me, I turn to see her questioning glance, hiding behind wire-framed glasses.

She asks, "Have you decided on a science fair project?" I look down at my hands, but they lack a suitable answer.

The 4th-grade science fair was a year-long project hosted in the gymnasium, complete with parents, faculty, and friends walking around the room, examining the culmination of your life's work. At least the depth of what we could create in the first ten years of life.

I was hopeful.

Deep inside, we all wanted to receive the coveted first-place ribbon. But as weeks passed from fall to winter, my topic eluded me. In those days, we didn't have Google or the internet to answer our most pressing questions. We were left to imagine the opportunities as our minds explored all possible areas, or we checked out a book in the library!

After several weeks of dreaming and searching through reference books for potential topics, I sat with the crushing feeling that I had no idea what to do. I did, however, have one question I wanted to answer.

Mrs. Stanley kept trinkets and treasures in her classroom. Models, graphs, and games surrounded the windows that overlooked the playground. In one tiny portion of the window, near the back of the room, sat four small aluminum cans. In their former life, they held various types of vegetables. Several years before, they were cleaned and converted into an astrological discovery zone. Painted to resemble a black kaleidoscope, you could pick them up, look toward the light, and see the Big Dipper, Little Dipper, and other constellations etched inside the ends of each metal can. I spent hours looking through them as I imagined how the constellations were made.

When it came time to answer her question, I looked up nervously and said, "I'd like to find out where constellations come from." With a combination of pleasantry and pride, she stared back in silence.

I remember her resignation, "Well," she said, "I don't think we can do that," as care twinkled in her eyes.

I was defeated, but she continued, "That question might be too tough to answer." With the gravity and grace of a teacher etched with years of training and a heart for learning, she helped me frame the question differently.

She said, "Why don't you explain what constellations _are_ and not specifically _where_ they come from? That would be a great science project." I contemplated her offering and nodded my head.

I agreed to try.

Today, I still remember the defeated feeling of being unable to answer the question. If I could employ a pensieve, I would return to my 10-year-old mind, like Albus Dumbledore in Harry Potter, and I'd siphon my excess thoughts. I'd pour them into an opal basin and examine them at leisure. If I could do that, I wonder what I would see.

I know this much. I wanted to know where constellations came from, but it wasn't the right question at the time. I learned to ask the right question.

Asking the Right Question

Purpose is such an elusive creature. It seems to twist and turn like a forest whose architect is unseen to the naked eye. But we must learn to ask different questions in our quest for purpose.

The vast majority of people seek to have a purpose in life. It's normal. But do we fully understand why? Do we understand how that pursuit causes anxiety and doubt? More importantly, do we recognize when it pulls us away from God

DO WE RECOGNIZE WHEN IT PULLS US AWAY FROM GOD AND NOT TOWARD HIM?

and not toward Him? We can only do that as we explore the paradox of purpose.

Exploring Purpose

For 25 years, research has fueled our language, writing, culture, and perspective about our quest for purpose. Scholars and researchers recently began identifying the benefits of having a sense of purpose. Their targeted focus led to the development of a new field of study called *Positive Psychology*, which examines human strengths and virtues.

The discovery started in 1998. At the time, Martin Seligman, president of the American Psychological Association, urged the psychology community to create a new direction of psychology that focused on adopting a perspective about human potential, motives, and capacities.[3]

He challenged them to ask different questions.

Before his prompting, psychologists mainly focused on treating mental illness and distress. The aftermath of two world wars necessitated researchers to focus on the trauma of soldiers across the globe who struggled with the effects of combat. After World War I, the United States became more aware of mental health problems[4] and focused its studies on treating the negative impact of trauma.

However, in the late 1990s, through the development of Positive Psychology, mental health experts began researching the factors that enable human beings to climb out of life's valleys. They sought to learn how to help people reach the summits of life's highest peaks.[5]

They sought to help people answer deep questions like "What is my purpose?"

The Purpose Paradox

The "What is my purpose?" question plagues people of all generations. Both a 15-year-old freshman and a 50-year-old freelancer ask this question at some point in their lives.

But the pursuit of purpose is a paradox like nothing else.

A paradox, by definition, has contradictory qualities that initially seem true. For instance, consider the contradictions in George Orwell's *1984*[6] novel, where he explains:

- War is peace.
- Freedom is slavery.
- Ignorance is strength.

Each is an example of a paradox. The ancient Greeks knew a paradox could take us outside our usual thinking as we considered a figure of speech that seemed to contradict itself.

I like words. They bring me peace. I often tell my husband that I am a "Worder." It's not a real term, but one I've created to capture my love for words. And I can imagine the ancient Greeks sitting around a stone table, trying to combine letters to identify the magnitude of what they were experiencing. They were "Worders," too.

When they authored this specific solution, they combined the prefix *para-* (which means "beyond" or "outside") with the verb *dokein* (which means "to think"). This allowed them to form the word *para doxos*, which means "contrary to expectation."

In the 1500s, English speakers borrowed the noun *paradoxum* from their Latin friends and created the word *paradox*.[7] Thus, it became the word we hear today.

The pursuit of purpose is a paradox: it is, by its nature, contrary to expectation. But despite the challenge it holds, we, as both Christians and secular humans, are obsessed with it.

The Obsession of Purpose

Today, at an alarming rate, Christians seem to be asking, "What is my purpose?" and pursuing it like a cat chasing a mouse. The more we hunt for it, the more anxious and doubtful we become.

But why?

- Is it because we strive to be good stewards of our time, talents, and treasures? *Absolutely.*
- Is it because, in recent years, we've watched the world turn upside down with global pandemics and disasters while feeling more isolated and alone? *Definitely.*
- Could it be something more profound, like deception, idolatry, or fear? *Possibly.*

Despite the shift in our perspective, the pursuit of purpose has existed for eternity. Humans have been asking, "What is my purpose?" since the beginning of time. We've only begun to explore and examine the psychology of it within the last 100 years.

The Psychology of Purpose

Before the 1970s, there was limited research on pursuing purpose. Victor Frankel wrote about man's quest for meaning in his post-holocaust research.[8] As a psychotherapist and former prisoner at Auschwitz and two satellite camps of Dachau, Viennese, his research and unique perspectives shaped the academic community while trying to define the psychological elements of purpose.

For years, Dr. Frankl suffered in the Nazi concentration camps. He used those experiences to help thousands of people by discovering *logotherapy*, a psychological treatment called "existential analysis." In this practice, he weaved the slender threads of a broken life into a firm pattern of meaning and responsibility.[9]

During his treatments, he asked his patients, "Why did you not commit suicide?" In their answers, he found a guideline that he used to braid their lives back together.[10] His research sparked a sixty-year exploration of this concept we call "purpose."

Scientists, philosophers, and theologians all try to describe it. Religious groups each define it in a slightly different way. The John Templeton Foundation report on the *Psychology of Purpose* explains:

> *"Over the past 20 years, the focus and scientific attention to purpose has increased dramatically. Before this, researchers largely believed that it was impossible to investigate a multifaceted and complex construct. Purpose is admittedly challenging to study."[11]*

Like joy, hope, peace, or love, *purpose* is difficult to define.

Defining Purpose

According to Webster,[12] *purpose* is often used in two contexts.

- First, it is an **object or end to be attained.**
- Second, it's a **subject under discussion or an action in execution.**

Both definitions can apply to our pursuit of purpose. But that definition alone doesn't give us the entire understanding of our meaning when we say "purpose."

Further explained by psychologists at Berkley University,[13] purpose is the *"abiding intention to achieve a **long-term goal** that is both **personally meaningful** and makes a **positive mark on the world.***"

The definition of purpose varies, to certain degrees, across cultures and religions. But a consensus has emerged across the academic community. Purpose includes three distinct elements.

The Elements of Purpose

Purpose typically includes three specific elements:[14]

1. **a goal** that is
2. **personally meaningful** and
3. inspired to make a difference in the world **beyond oneself.**

In this definition, a person's *purpose* is more than a state of being or belief. To fully realize or achieve *purpose*, our definition must include a **goal or tangible outcome** that one can identify.

And therein lies another problem.

As Christians, we seek to define our purpose in a specific concept that encapsulates our entire lives. Take our careers, for example. We often consider one primary role, vocation, or task we believe we are divinely inspired to pursue.

- Will I be a doctor?
- Will I join the military?
- Do I want to have children?
- Will I serve in full-time ministry?

But those questions are more about our roles throughout our lifetime than our overarching purpose. Our roles will vary across the seasons of our lives.

At times, we try to organize all our actions into a neat, clean package called *purpose*. We find ourselves frustrated or overwhelmed when we can't.

We look at the world and compare ourselves to those who seem to have it all together. We think they must have found their purpose, so what's wrong with me? In some ways, we believe that purpose is divinely given and issued at the time when our souls were created. And that God has given each of us one specific thing we're supposed to do for our entire lives: *our sole purpose.*

But is that true? It's confusing, to say the least. The confusion stems from our flawed perception and definition of purpose.

Purpose vs. Meaning

> SOMETIMES, WE REPLACE THE WORD PURPOSE WITH OTHERS LIKE MEANING, CALLING, OR DESTINY. BUT THEY AREN'T THE SAME THING.

Sometimes, we replace the word *purpose* with others like *meaning*, *calling*, or *destiny*. But they aren't the same thing. Psychologists presume that when a person finds a "purpose in life," it represents a subset of various sources of meaning.

For example, people can find *meaning in life* by watching a shooting star. But they would find *purpose* when they work to preserve natural resources, fight terrorism, or strive to end poverty.

The meaning of one's life can be broad and includes values, ability, and perceptions of self-worth. It is also where people make sense of or see the significance in their lives.[15]

Meaning and purpose are different. According to positive psychologist Jonathan Haidt[16] when people ask to understand the meaning of life, they ask two different questions:

1. What is the purpose *of life?*
2. What is the purpose *within life?*

Through this lens, we can see how pursuing purpose quickly becomes complicated. When you ask, "What is my purpose?" are you asking about the purpose *of life* or *within life?*

Often, we ask both. But it seems that we're trying to use one question to find many answers. And then, when we mix purpose with goals, the answers get harder to find.

Goals vs. Purpose

If we go back to our previous definition, *purpose* includes three things: **a goal** that's **personally meaningful** and **beyond oneself.**

Goals are tangible. Goals can be quantified and measured. Many items can fill this block if you think about the various roles in your life.

Take my life, for example. I wear many hats. I'm a mom, wife, Christian, veteran, military spouse, daughter, sister, writer, founder, and podcaster. If I look at my life and the roles I've held, I can identify many goals, dreams, and callings that I've had or pursued.

Over the years, I've wanted to do lots of things:

- Write a book
- Love my children well
- Learn to crochet
- Get out of debt
- Start a nonprofit
- Live on a tropical island paradise
- SCUBA dive the Great Barrier Reef
- Travel to outer space (I'm still holding out for this one, Elon Musk)
- Run a marathon (which didn't last very long, by the way)

The list goes on and on. Each goal is personally meaningful, and many have an impact beyond me. But my purpose, as a woman of faith, is not contingent upon one or all of those things. Those are simply goals that I've had along my life's journey.

Do you see the difference? At times, those goals came from a place of passion: an interest I found or something that brought meaning to me. But they aren't *my purpose*. They're just things I've done.

Before we dig further into the psychology of purpose, let's see what the Scriptures say.

Finding Purpose in the Bible

When I started this journey to define "purpose," I first went to the back of the book for the answer. I opened my English Standard Version Study Bible and searched for purpose in the index.

But I came up empty-handed. Then I dug into the Old and New Testament theology reference library I've retained from previous graduate school classes, and again, I came up with nothing.

So, I began to search for all the places where the word *purpose* was used in the Scriptures. I found it 226 times across 25 different word translations. That, my friend, is confusing.

We commonly use certain verses in the Bible as references for our Christian purpose questions, so let's begin with Romans 8:28.

According to God's Purpose

"And we know that for those who love God, all things work together for good, for those who are called according to his purpose"
(Romans 8:28).[17]

In Romans 8:28, purpose is translated as *prothesin*. The root word is *protithemai*, defined as either (1) *a setting forth*[18] or (2) a *purpose*. In this context, *prothesin* is used three other times in the New Testament.

- Ephesians 1:11, Paul explains that we have obtained an inheritance and been predestined according to the *purpose of the One* who works all things according to the *counsel of His will* so that we who were the first to hope in Christ might be *to the praise of his glory.*

- In Ephesians 3:11, Paul continues to explain that his *purpose* is to preach to the Gentiles and to bring to light the plan of the mystery hidden for all ages in God, who created all things, so that the church, *through the manifold wisdom of God*, might be made known to rules and authorities in heavenly places. It is also *according to the* eternal purpose *that He realized in Christ Jesus, in whom we have boldness and access with confidence through our faith in him* (v11–13). We'll come back to those references in a moment.

- In 2 Timothy 1:9, Paul explains that the One who saved and called us holy did it not according to our works, but by *His own purpose* and grace, having been given us in Christ Jesus before time eternal.

Throughout the Scriptures, we see a common theme as we unpack the definition of purpose. Each element in the previous examples shows us that **God** defines the purpose, not man. And that purpose is **found in Christ alone.**

So, therein lies the greatest and most deceptive problem regarding our quest for purpose. Do you see it? Let's revisit Romans 8:28. It says, *"And we know that in all things God works for the good of those who love him, who have been called <u>according to his purpose.</u>"*

In this verse, we find the key to our hidden purpose door. It says, *"according to His purpose."* God's purpose, not ours. Not our interpretation nor our biased perspectives. His purpose alone is the answer.

So, what is God's purpose for our lives? We have a divine purpose in Christ, but that question is often difficult to answer. Isaiah explains why we struggle.

Understanding the Ways of God

In the book of Isaiah, we learn that the Lord's thoughts are not ours. "For my thoughts are not your thoughts, neither are your ways my ways, declares the Lord" (Isaiah 55:8–9). We don't know the plans or ways of the Lord, but we do know certain things:

- We know a divine, sovereign God created us.[19]
- We know God sees the Church without spot or blemish.[20]
- We know we've been set apart, created in His image, for "His good works."[21]
- We know He gave us a Great Commission and Commandment to live our lives.[22]
- We know God calls us to love Him and to love the world.[23]

Let's revisit the greatest commandment that Jesus gave us.

The Great Commandment

Jesus traveled the countryside, teaching many about the love of God. In one session, the Pharisees and Sadducees were gathered together. Scripture tells us that one of them, a lawyer, tested

Jesus with a question. He asked, "Teacher, what is the greatest commandment in the Law?"

Jesus replied:[24]

> *You shall love the Lord your God with all your heart and with all your soul and with all your mind. This is the great and first commandment. And a second is like it: You shall love your neighbor as yourself.*

Moses first gave that commandment to the Israelites. In Deuteronomy 6:4, the *Shema* was decreed. We'll explore its foundation more in Chapter 3, but for now, remember that Jesus gave the commandment to the people as an instruction for their lives. Everything rested on this challenge. And in that, our purpose is simple.

God tells us two things:

1. to love Him with all of your heart, soul, and mind
2. to love your neighbor as yourself.[25]

Our purpose as Christians remains the same: we are called to love God and the world. And that, friend, can be done in a billion different ways. But I will submit that if the answer is so simple, why do we struggle? Because our pursuit of purpose is often focused on ourselves rather than God.

We take our eyes off God when we focus on ourselves. You can only truly focus on one thing at a time. When

WHY DO WE STRUGGLE? BECAUSE OUR PURSUIT OF PURPOSE IS OFTEN FOCUSED ON OURSELVES RATHER THAN GOD.

we take our eyes off the Father, we lose sight of what guides and sustains us.

Shifting Our Focus

Take the story of Peter, for example. In the Gospel of Matthew, we find the lesson Jesus taught the disciples about faith. The disciples were in the boat, crossing the sea. Jesus left them and went up the mountains to pray. When he returned that evening, their boat had already left the shore.

In the early morning hours, sometime between 3–6 a.m., Jesus approached the disciples. As the wind blew and the boat rocked across the dark, open sea, the disciples saw the image of a person walking upon the water, and they were afraid. The Scripture says:

But immediately, Jesus spoke to them, saying, "Take heart; it is I. Do not be afraid." And Peter answered, "Lord, if it is you, command me to come to you on the water." He said, "Come." So, Peter exited the boat, walked on the water, and came to Jesus. But when he saw the wind, he was afraid and beginning to sink; he cried out, "Lord, save me." Jesus immediately reached out his hand and took hold of him, saying, "O you of little faith, why did you doubt?" [26]

When Peter stopped looking at Jesus, he started to fall. Jesus didn't lay out a 5-point plan in the water. He simply said, "Come." And Peter took one step toward the Savior.

Do you see the simplicity of it? Peter took one step toward the Savior. That's all he needed to understand. That's all Jesus asked him to do.

Taking Your First Step

It takes time to dig into and decipher God's Word. It takes intention to learn how to walk with the Savior. But that discovery journey is the process. As my friend Mike says, "The journey is the destination."

What if the pursuit of purpose, as we know and see it in the Christian world today, is an idol? What if we're using this as another device to say, "Lord, what about ME is important?" Instead of saying, "Lord, what about you?"

What if God has already told us our purpose? I believe He has—and it's simple, friend—love Him and love the world.

But it's not easy, is it? If that's the answer, then why do we struggle so much?

When our focus shifts from the One who created the world with His breath, a sovereign and divine God, to us, we miss our holy guide standing in front of us every day.

We miss His promises in all things.

God's promises are the guideposts we need to live a life *fully alive* in Him. We have a divine purpose ordained by God. The answer has already been given to us: love me and love the world. But navigating the weight and burden of purpose is backbreaking.

When we learn how to see His promises, we can unwrap His truth. That revelation allows us to see the world from a different perspective. We ask different questions to clarify our pursuit of purpose, and by changing our focus, we learn how to let all of God live through every part of us.

That *is* our purpose.

A Prayer to Lay Down the Burden of Purpose

Dear Lord,

Thank You for offering me a fresh perspective on purpose. Today, I lay down my past expectations. I offer them to You as a symbol of my willingness to seek Your face. May I always focus on You, Lord, instead of myself. And may I be willing to "Come" when You call me.

Thank you for Your heart. May I fix my eyes upon You, finding my purpose in Your love.

Amen

THE ANXIETY OF PURPOSE

Our anxiety does not empty tomorrow of its sorrows,
but only empties today of its strengths.

—C. H. Spurgeon

Have you ever tried to catch the sunshine? When my youngest daughter was small, she spent hours mesmerized by the tiny dust particles that floated through our house on a bright, clear day. She called them "sun fuzzies" and fervently tried to catch them. She'd sway back and forth, with her soft, blond curls draping around her shoulders, as she looked at them with wonder.

Countless times, I watched her reach up with silent anticipation, trying to catch them. But when she opened her tiny hands, they were empty of the treasure she hoped to claim.

When I think about purpose or seek to define it, I see a girl standing in front of a long, tall window, looking across the vast green world, swaying back and forth, trying to catch her purpose before it floats away.

Defining purpose can be like trying to catch the sunshine. You can't hold the rays in your hand, but you can reach out and feel the warmth of it on your face.

Purpose gives us hope. It fuels us to move forward despite our hardships. The same can be said for faith, love, or grace. It's proven that we, as humans, need a sense of purpose in our lives. Pursuing purpose often causes anxiety, fear, disbelief, and doubt. But despite the pain it causes, we still hunger for it.

Our Need for Purpose

I've worked with many people as a business coach, ministry leader, and mentor. When clients consider a career change or want to start a business or nonprofit, they often say they want to "help people" and for their life to have "meaning or purpose."

But why?

Victor Frankl proposed that everyone is motivated to discover their life's purpose. Without it, we experience feelings of meaninglessness and emptiness, which are often associated with depression and boredom.[27] Purpose provides a powerful sense of direction. It helps others and enhances our well-being.

We strive to live out our authentic purpose through our vocation or other roles that allow us to use our gifts. That brings us a deep sense of worth or value, believing we contributed to the common good.[28] Purpose also gives us the confidence to use our lives to help others feel loved, seen, and valued.

In 2009, researchers Kasddan and McKnight studied the origins of purpose, hoping to offer insight into how and why certain people are healthy and prosperous in the long-term quest for purpose.[29] They explain that "a purpose provides a bedrock foundation that allows a person to be more resilient to obstacles, stress, and strain."[30]

As mentioned before, we need a sense of purpose in our lives. It fuels us. It gives us focus, clarity, and a vision for our future. But if we unwrap the psychology of purpose, we'll see how that need comes from a deeper place. It's not simply driven by our desire to improve the world or be good stewards of our lives.

There are two reasons why pursuing purpose is so important to us.

1) First, we need to *identify what drives us.*

2) Second, we need to *bring order to our lives.*

The search for purpose *is the innermost circle of what drives you.*[31] Purpose helps us cast a positive vision for our future.[32] When we're uncertain about something, we experience confusion. Confusion brings anxiety, hesitancy, doubt, and fear. Having an overall sense of purpose in our lives gives us vision and focus. If we can see where we're going or believe that our challenges are part of a "greater plan," we can find the strength to endure tiring times.

> THE SEARCH FOR PURPOSE IS THE INNERMOST CIRCLE OF WHAT DRIVES YOU.

The Pain of Purpose

The search for purpose impacts more than high school students or college graduates. Every age struggles at various intervals in their lives. And if I'm honest, that concerns me. As a lover of humans, the more profound challenge for me is seeing the agony on their faces. I often watch clients and friends wrestle with the pain and psychological distress as they try to answer their purpose questions.

The same has been true in my own life. Over the years, I watched others work, write, and worship, believing they had found their purpose and that I was passed over. I never considered how much my desire for purpose was driven and guided by a social construct.

We learn by watching others. If you're a parent, you know this well. As your children grow, they mimic everything you do, both good and bad! It's how we learn.

So, when we look at our quest for purpose, we see it everywhere. We believe—or we've been told to believe—that we should chase, define, and capitalize on it.

But is that what God intended us to do?

We spend our days overwhelmed with life. We serve, live, and acquire everything we believe is required. We eat organic foods, sleep 8 hours, read our Bible, serve in ministry, pursue a fulfilling job, etc. The list goes on and on.

But the more we try to discover our purpose, the more complex life seems to get. It's like trying to find the pot of gold at the end of the rainbow. Once we get there, we see how the light doesn't touch the ground. There is no treasure waiting to be found. The rays of light expand just beyond the ridgeline. And so, we fall onto the damp grass, disappointed and exhausted.

We grieve.

After time passes, we stand up, dust off our knees, and resolve to continue walking toward the edge of the earth, searching for our hidden purpose treasure. We believe it may be hidden in a different place, and our pursuit of purpose quickly becomes overwhelming. We find ourselves filled with worry and doubt. We feel the pressure to find our purpose, which leaves us with anxiety and confusion.

Defining Purpose Anxiety

Unfortunately, pursuing a purpose doesn't always bring happiness or peace. In 2014, Larissa Rainey coined the phrase "purpose anxiety"[33] in her capstone project titled, *The Search for Purpose in Life: An Exploration of Purpose, the Search Process and Purpose Anxiety,* as she tried to explain the basis for our negative feelings when we try to find or pursue our purpose in life.

Larissa explains how the pursuit of purpose leaves us confused, insecure, overwhelmed, powerless, and responsible for the outcomes of our lives.[34] We feel the pressure to be good stewards of our lives, resources, finances, and gifts, but that pressure ultimately causes us to feel apprehension and fear.

But why?

The answer lies beneath the surface of the great *purpose iceberg*. It's hidden in our identity, our need for control, our desire to conform to society's standards, and our tendency to compare ourselves to others.

The Iceberg of Purpose

Have you heard the analogy that a problem is like an iceberg? The depth is unclear. The pursuit of purpose is like an iceberg. We see a jagged top peering above the waterline but fail to comprehend what lies beneath the surface.

Humans are complex beings. Using the iceberg analogy, we often only see our actions or behaviors above the surface. We need to understand the factors that motivate our behaviors. Those needs or fears sit below the brim, remaining unseen to the naked eye.

The Iceberg of Purpose

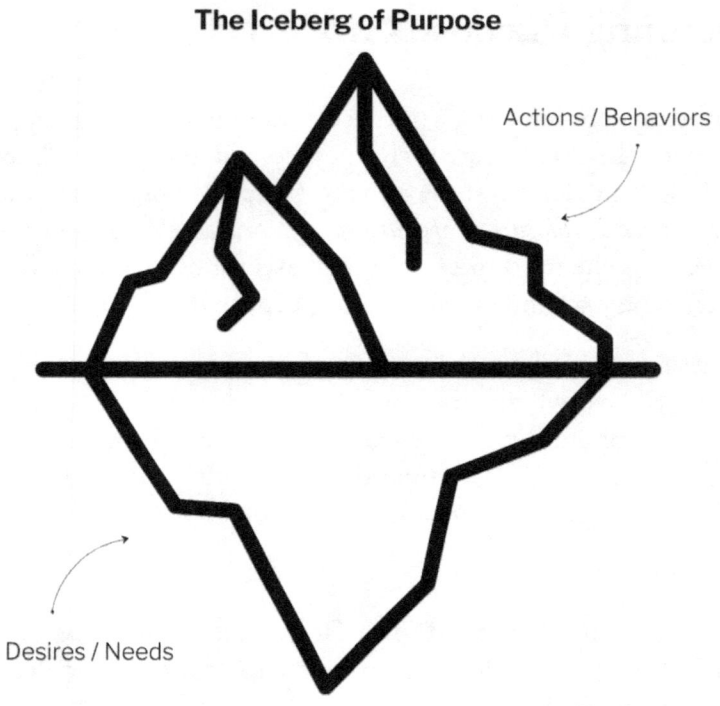

Actions / Behaviors

Desires / Needs

At the root of many behaviors is one driving force: *our identity*.

For years, social psychologists explored the concept of identity and investigated how our behaviors manifest in the world. Those social identity processes are at the core of their study.

They discovered that identity is both a psychological and social concept. To unwrap our need for purpose, we must first understand ourselves.

Imagine our identity as a peanut butter and jelly sandwich. We have two pieces of bread. One half is our **self-concept,** or how we see ourselves. The second half contains **the social self**, which is how we appear to others. Combine those with our **self-esteem,** which is like the peanut butter and jelly that holds everything together. Using this example, we can deconstruct the source that feeds our anxiety of purpose.

Don't worry—I'll explain each of them. Let's start with the self-concept first!

The Self-Concept

The *self-concept* is what we think about ourselves. It influences our thoughts, feelings, and behaviors.[35] Researchers believe that our sense of self emerges in childhood and is derived from social interactions.

Take the example of a looking glass. Often, other people serve as a mirror in which we see ourselves. In his 1943 research, George Herbert Mead explained that we often come to know ourselves by *imagining what significant others think of us* and then incorporating this perception into our self-concepts.[36] We create the concept of who we are. Our identity is shaped by what we believe people think about us.

I'm a writer. I'm a warrior. I am wounded.

How we see ourselves guides our vision for our lives, behaviors, and understanding of purpose. Identity and purpose, if you've not already noticed, are linked tightly together. They'd be tied in a knot if they were two pieces of string.

Other psychologists claim that the self is relational, meaning we draw our sense of who we are from our past and current relationships with significant others.[37]

Can you see how self-concept fuels and guides our perception of our purpose?

Now, let's move on to the second element: *our social self.*

The Social Self

The social self is how we receive recognition from others. Both are relevant in pursuing purpose because we carry identity standards and self-perceptions, whether we consciously identify them or not.

When we connect our definition of purpose with our social self, we believe our roles or how we show up in the world are our principal values. It shifts our perspective and beliefs about ourselves.

Lastly, our self-esteem heavily influences our perception of our identity and purpose.

Still with me? Great, we'll dig into self-esteem next, and I promise not to ask you to relive your most embarrassing experiences!

Self-Esteem

We've all navigated the trials of self-esteem. Visit any middle school cafeteria, and you'll see history's deepest, hardest season of self-esteem management. I remember my parents telling me not to worry about what other people thought of me. But it was harder than they described.

How we define our self-esteem is an internal identity concept. We measure two elements: how we see ourselves as we exist (now) and how we want to see ourselves (tomorrow).

For example, if I think I need to lose weight, I imagine my current self (how much I weigh today) compared to my future self (how much I should weigh tomorrow). I have a negative self-esteem if I weigh more today than I should.

Conversely, I will have positive self-esteem if I consider my future weight will be greater than I weigh today. Today, I believe I am doing better than tomorrow, so I am content.

Can you see how this example applies to purpose? When we compare where we are today versus where we believe we should be tomorrow, we experience either a positive or negative emotion. If I think I'm not living my "purpose," then I will carry a negative anxiety or feeling about my identity and my life.

Psychologists developed a simple exercise to help you practice this concept of self.

Consider writing down five traits that describe how you are. Then, beside that list, write down the five traits describing the person you think you ought to be. That simple exercise allows you to identify what psychologists call your "actual self vs. your ideal self."

At the end of Part 1 of this book, I offer space to walk through that exercise so you can see it in action. But for now, we acknowledge that we **all** have **unmet expectations** about who we are. The problem with these elements is that our perception of well-being is tied to our sense of identity and how we perceive our purpose.

Searching for Purpose

If you believe you haven't found your purpose, you'll keep looking for it. If someone says you should be looking for one, you'll stop and say, "Yes, I do need one," and continue searching for it. That search causes anxiety and doubt because you will believe you're missing something.

WE DERIVE OUR IDENTITY, VALUE, AND WORTH FROM OUR PURPOSE.

Do you see the deception and the destruction of that challenge? Our efforts to "pursue my purpose" link directly to our identity and how we see ourselves. We derive our identity, value, and worth from our *purpose*. We consider whether we've achieved it or how we should live according to it. The tension or anxiety we feel is based on our perception or the belief that a gap exists.

But does it? Is there a gap? Or has your purpose already been defined?

A Reason to Refocus

Every person wants to be significant. We desire to be seen and heard. We long to be fully loved, for one person to see us in our raw and vulnerable design and to love and accept us just as we are. But that desire starts with the Father and can only be truly filled with the Father's love.

Often, we let our self-interest guide our journey. We focus on our self-limitations and self-doubt. When we shift our focus onto ourselves, we start to see how the framework of our lives changes. Our goals shift. We become obsessed with them. It's a never-ending cycle.

So, why does all of this matter? When we have expectations of ourselves and think we're not living up to those standards, we experience negative emotions and suffer from excessive fears and anxiety. If there is a mismatch between our actual and ideal selves, we feel disappointed, frustrated, unfulfilled, and sad.[38]

The self, the social self, and self-esteem guide our feelings and thoughts about our identity and pursuit of purpose.

But it's not solely our fault. Consider our focus and influences. When we look at the world, what do we see? We see those we love and trust encouraging us to find our purpose. We feel the weight and pressure of it. We feel pushed to decide how we want to spend every waking moment of our lives. Purpose. Productivity. Platform. But that is not how God works. God works in the moments of every day. The gentle whisper as we sit on the edge of the hospital bed, holding onto our loved one's hands. He shows us His purpose in the beautiful comfort that comes after the deepest pain.

If the world and the church tell you to find your purpose, you'll naturally look at everyone else, thinking they have it, and you don't. We become discouraged and frustrated and focus on those around us rather than seeing the promises of God standing in front of us every day.

That's why it's so important for us to refocus our perspective of purpose. We must recognize our desire for control, conformance, and comparison as factors influencing our behavior and beliefs about purpose.

Cultural Conformance

In today's culture, we're surrounded by signs, t-shirts, and sermons telling us to find our purpose. But is that even possible? The quest to identify our life's purpose goes deeper than calling, identity, jobs, ministry, roles, or even suffering.

As Christians, we sometimes struggle to live fully present. The "What is my purpose?" question seems to be in every sermon, story, and study group. And when life gets busy or complicated, we can't find the ways to unwrap our purpose equation to try and find our personal, uniquely designed hidden treasure that we believe God placed in the world just for us.

Our purpose questions come from large and small areas of our lives combined. Their intersection seems wrapped like a ball of yarn, leaving us unable to see where one part starts or stops. We start by asking, "What is my purpose?" But then, along life's journey, we gather other questions about purpose as the years pass. We revisit the same question when life hits heavy or we lose friends, jobs, faith, health, children, dreams, and joy.

We don't often see how our purpose question combines many other questions. If the purpose question was one that God intended for us to ask, then why do we struggle so much?

Society and psychologists offer many theories for what motivates us to search for purpose. Identifying what drives Christians should be simple. It's the gospel, right? That's easy. But if our purpose questions were simple, we'd have much smaller books and clearer sermons.

If the Church lived a life of divine purpose, people could open the tops of our chapels and peer inside, seeing people fully alive, living wholly in Him, and being salt and light to the world. However, when I speak with people across various landscapes, industries, and ministries, they often reach the same crossroads. They question their purpose and struggle to find it.

Control

Our quest for answering the purpose question is rooted in a profound need for control. For peace. For order. That's how the human brain is designed. Our brain organizes information. It categorizes and files moments and memories into bins so we can make sense of them.

When something new or disorganized comes our way, our brain attempts to file it in a known location. We try to determine whether it's safe or harmful. We consider if we should stay or go. Fight, Flight, Freeze.

When our life events and circumstances change, they influence how we see or try to answer our purpose questions. Our perspective shifts as we experience the trials and tribulations of life. Eventually, our purpose questions become crowded with other questions about loss, pain, and suffering. We question the purpose of layoffs, pandemics, suffering, cancer diagnosis, and abuse, just to name a few. What is the point if we can't find a purpose in the pain?

Comparison

We also have a deep need to compare ourselves to others. Again, the social self-element of our identity is at play.

Here's an example. Meet my friend, John. John believes his purpose is to be a doctor. But, over time, he has become more agitated and frustrated with his life. He looks at peers and colleagues and desires a greater sense of fulfillment. At the end of a long day, he sits with his wife and asks, "What is the point, Sarah?" She rests her hand on his and listens with compassion.

As a Christian, John believes in the sovereignty and grace of God. But he's so focused on completing the tasks in front of him each day or comparing himself to others that he forgets that his identity and value are more significant than his title or bank account.

Today's society considers John's quest admirable, even righteous. He helps people. He's achieved a daunting goal. So, why is he frustrated? Why does John struggle?

He isn't alone. Research shows that pursuing purpose leaves many people struggling with psychological distress.[39] But it doesn't have to be this way. John's focus on his *purpose* needs to change.

The Idol of Purpose

If we use purpose as our sole focus, life becomes unbearable. If the purpose is our goal post, vision, and destination, we measure everything to that standard. We focus on ourselves instead of the sovereign God. When we do that, we quickly lose sight of the most important thing: His love.

Like Peter, where we focus matters. The world's noise melts away when we fix our eyes upon Jesus. Our focus guides our perspectives. We find God's peace by allowing the light of His promises to reveal hidden parts of our hearts and minds.

So, friend, what if we're asking the wrong question? What if the question "What is my purpose?" is part of a greater, deeper, more mystical, and hard-to-define understanding?

Are we trying to solve our "What is my purpose?" problem, or are we trying to satisfy a more profound desire? I think the answer is the second. How do we know what that is? We have to look deeper at the question in later chapters.

At a deeper level, many believe that the gift of life includes the responsibility to find and achieve your unique capacity for greatness.[40] It's a normal human desire, like love. But as Christians, we are called to shift our focus. When we stand on a different summit, the view and focus change. We learn to find value in other things. It's a matter of perspective. We learn that our identity is found in Christ alone.

Through the last few years of pandemics and world events, it's easy to see how we grasp every straw to find the answer to our "What is my purpose?" questions. But we seem to be asking it more urgently, in desperation. It fuels our sermons and situations. Books, podcasts, and conversations are all focused on the topic. Are we more transparent or confident with all this information being shared worldwide? My answer is no.

Which causes me to ask these fundamental questions:

- Are we looking at God or ourselves?
- Is our pursuit of purpose more about ourselves, or are we on a quest to find God's peace and provision in our everyday lives?
- Are we taking one step toward the Savior? If you answer yes, you're ready to discover how to find God's divine purpose and promises waiting for you.

A Prayer for Laying Down the Anxiety of Purpose

Dear Lord,

Thank You for the promises You've set into eternity long before I walked this earth or breathed air into my lungs. You are sovereign, and I surrender my pursuit into Your hands. Today, I lay down my ideas and notions of purpose and ask You to replace all worry, doubt, and fear with the peace to know that my identity is in You. Allow Your peace to wash over me each day.

Amen.

GOD'S PERFECT PLAN

"You can see God from anywhere
if your mind is set to love and obey Him."

- A.W. Tozer

What comes to mind when you think of God's sovereignty and strength? Is it something audacious, like parting the Red Sea or giving sight to a blind man? Maybe it's how the people of Israel were protected for 40 years as they wandered through the wilderness, how God shut the mouths of lions, or, lest we not forget, the greatest miracle: the birth and resurrection of Jesus Christ.

The Bible is filled with miraculous stories of God's power and glory. While these stories are impressive and, at times, hard for our human minds to comprehend, there is another side to God's miracles—one that is less dramatic but life-changing nonetheless.

The Scriptures record countless instances of angels appearing in human form to help a person in need. We discover God's magnificent power and mercy in both complex and ordinary things.

God is not solely concerned about your quest for purpose. He wants your heart with all its delicate and doubtful pieces. To find peace during our purpose journey, we surrender our hearts to His divine will. We do this by trusting in two foundational elements:

1) God is sovereign.

2) You are made in His image.

Before releasing the most fragile parts of our purpose journey, we must accept God has a divine purpose, knit together by His sovereign hand.

His Sovereign Hand

How you experience God's purpose in the world is a daily adventure waiting to be discovered. The revelation of each step only comes from one trustworthy source: Jesus.

Our Source of Truth

Jesus shared many decrees with the disciples. He spoke to crowds about John the Baptist, the judgment of unrepentant cities, and how only the Son of God knows the Father.[41] Jesus told them that no one knows the Father except the Son and anyone to whom the Son reveals to him.[42]

In His teachings, God gave us the foundation for our purpose question: **Everything from God is revealed through the Son, Jesus Christ.**

- Jesus is loving.
- He is gracious.
- He comforts those who suffer.
- He provides for those in need.
- He redeems us with His everlasting love.

Jesus is all these things, and we are not. The cornerstone of our purpose question is found in *Him*.

But that's not enough, is it? That one simple answer isn't enough. It doesn't keep us from being discouraged or confused when we look at our life, examine the pain of our past, and try to find the confidence that we're stewarding the gifts God has given us. At times, the weight of it is daunting.

Christians struggle—maybe more so than those in the secular world—because we feel the weight of responsibility. We carry the burden of purpose. We acknowledge that the purpose paradox overwhelms us. We struggle when we look at the vast array of our lives, the sea of unmet expectations, broken promises, and endless opportunities.

A key reason for our distress is our failure to see God's hand upon our lives. Take heart, friend! God offered us a commandment that covers our concerns.

Hear O Israel

We process everything through the lens and life of Christ: the gospel. We believe in one true God and rest our faith foundation in the *Shema*. Moses first gave this degree to the Israelites.[43] It is a short passage but contains the commandments that bind God's promises to His chosen people.

> *"Hear, O Israel: The Lord our God, the Lord is one. You shall love the Lord your God with all your heart, soul, and might. These words I command today shall be on your heart."*

Because we are God's chosen people, with an election long before our birth, God claimed us as His treasured possessions and set His love upon us.[44] Moses teaches us that "the Lord our God *is*

God, faithful to keep a covenant and steadfast love with those who love Him and keep His commandments."[45]

In his teachings, Jesus reminds us there is one God, **the head, YHWH. His sovereignty reigns above all else.**

Paul reminds us of this truth: *But we know that there is only one God, the Father, who created all things[a] and made us to be his own; and one Lord Jesus Christ, who made everything and gives us life.*[46]

R. Walter L. Moberly, English theologian and professor at Durham University, cautions Christians if they gloss over the miracle of this statement. At times, Christians can become "dulled to the often-astonishing implications due to their common knowledge of famous biblical passages".[47] My interpretation of his statement is that, if we're not careful, we can miss God standing in front of us every, single day.

> **IF WE'RE NOT CAREFUL, WE CAN MISS GOD STANDING IN FRONT OF US EVERY, SINGLE DAY.**

When we sit with the Scriptures, we must allow ourselves to be transported into the pages before us. We know the rest of the story, but the transformation Moses and the Israelites experienced must have been a miracle.

Missing the Miracle

Imagine Moses passing along this decree to the Israelites. He met face-to-face with YHWH, the great I AM. In this intimate exchange, God appointed him as prophet and mediator for His people. Moberly reminds us how Moses is commanding the Israelites to remember the degrees of the Lord.[48]

The relationship between YHWH and Israel is unique, intimate, and one-of-a-kind. No other like it has been known. Rabbi Wolf Gunther Plaut explains this declaration of the *Shema* meant that God "undergirded all laws of nature and for mankind; hence heaven and earth, as well as human history, were His domain."[49] The exchange provides the beautiful tapestry on which our purpose rests. Without God's sovereignty, no other element matters.

For those who practice the Jewish faith, the *Shema* wraps their heart in an intimate and powerful assurance of the sovereignty of God.

Christians cling to the feet of Jesus, but our roots stem from the same place: God is sovereign.

And as we seek to unwrap our purpose questions, we are reminded that we have one primary charge, as Michael Fishbane, an American scholar of Judaism and rabbinic literature, explains. We are called to "affirm God in one's life, through mind and heart and deed, through teaching and interpretation everywhere.[50]

How we pursue our Christian life and find our purpose cannot be found in checklists or spreadsheets, even though I love both. It's rooted in finding peace, identity, and wholeness in God alone.

Our encounter with the love of our Savior, Jesus Christ, coupled with our belief and understanding of God's character, create the framework that holds together our life's foundation. Without these two cornerstones, nothing else matters.

When we ask, "What is my purpose?" we must start at the beginning. We stand on the foundation that we are made in God's image.

Fearfully and Wonderfully Made

We root all we are and do in the promise that God created us in His image, *the Imago Dei*. We trust that God came to earth as a fully divine and human man and sacrificed Himself for our salvation. God sent the Holy Spirit, thus forming the triune God, the Holy Trinity, to guide and sustain us.

Friend, you are made in the image of God.

Let that sink in for a moment.

Do you understand the weight of it?

Do you understand the power that it contains?

Without this foundational truth, the very framework of the Gospel is upended. If God loved us so much that He came to earth as a man to feel the way we feel, love the way we love, and hurt the way we hurt, His love can sustain us.

The question of purpose must be posed correctly. We must position our hearts and minds to see God's promises—not the question nor the situation surrounding us today. If we leave them too long, those things get cloudy, and we lose sight of the Savior. We fail to see the one they called Jesus of Nazareth—the Messiah.

We believe purpose is about us, our unique design, heart, will, and mind. And it indeed includes those elements, but only when we align ourselves under the arms and protection of the Savior.

But that can only be done with peace and confidence when we surrender our hearts to Him and begin to see and know that God loves us. Then, everything we do is done from the posture of overflowing love.

We give because He gave to us.

We love because He loves us.

We hope in His assurances despite what stands before us.

And we surrender to Him because, on broken nights, only His hope remains.

As Christians, we must reconcile the fact that He chose us. We are redeemed, surrendered, raptured, and peculiar. We don't always make sense to the world. If left to our own devices, we might believe this thing called "grace."

We employ the mantle of Christ and commit to His cause. "Yes, Lord, I will follow you. I will follow you with all that I have. I will give you all my life: heart, mind, soul, and strength."

We make that commitment, often without fully knowing or understanding the foundation of God's love. And then we fall exhausted into bed at night, praying for miracles, or we find ourselves lying on the cold tile of our bathroom floor, clinging to hope.

We strive to make our families and communities the best we can, but we are human. And on most days, we are left asking, "What is the point, anyway?"

Rooted in Love

As Christians, everything we do is rooted in one foundational principle: love. We rely on it, seek it, and collapse into it when the winds of life blow. Love promises that despite the storm or the pain we see, God will never leave us nor abandon us. God promises to love us forevermore.

In Jeremiah 31:3, God tells him, "I have loved you with an everlasting love." That promise, that one simple truth, guides all that we are and believe.

But what happens when life falls apart in front of us? What happens when you wake up holding the discharge paperwork from the emergency room visit that says *cancer*? What do you do when the doctor tells you the baby growing inside you cannot survive outside the womb, and you're faced with the most complex decisions of your life?

Instead of asking, "What is the purpose?" we shift our focus to God's promises.

Consider this:

1) What foundational promises keep us grounded when everything else disappears?
2) How do you focus on God's promises instead of searching for your life's purpose?

He is always and only the sovereign God; He is first and forevermore. We want to submit to God's authority. We seek the answers to our purpose questions, specifically and intimately. We wonder, "How do I make sense of my purpose?"

Dear friend, there is encouragement for those who seek the answer. We search for its meaning and the treasures it contains.

In Ephesians 3:13, Paul tells us, "Don't lose the heart of what he is suffering for us, which is for our glory."

For Your Glory

We talk a lot about the glory of God. We seek to honor His sovereignty in all things. But could God also be motivated by *our* glory? Not a glory that sits above nor equal to His own, but that which allows us, as His chosen people, to shine His light in dark places?

We know Paul suffered for our glory. But what does that mean?

In this passage, the Greek word for *glory* is [doxa], which means "a most glorious condition, most exalted state." It both refers to the condition of God the Father in heaven, to which Christ was raised after He completed His work on earth. It also represents the condition of blessedness, into which it is appointed and promised that true Christians shall enter after their Savior returns from heaven.

God's purpose for our lives, both here on earth and in eternity, includes our glory, which is the praise, honor, dignity, grace, and majesty of that which belongs to God.

Dear friend, you belong to God.

And in that act of adoption, you freely receive His promises for your life.

GOD'S PURPOSE FOR OUR LIVES, BOTH HERE ON EARTH AND IN ETERNITY, INCLUDES OUR GLORY, WHICH IS THE PRAISE, HONOR, DIGNITY, GRACE, AND MAJESTY OF THAT WHICH BELONGS TO GOD.

God's Promises

Ephesians 3:4, 6–12 tells us that we have been given the mystery of Christ that all Gentiles are fellow heirs, members of the same body, and receive the promise in Christ Jesus through the gospel.

We receive "unsearchable riches of Christ" according to the eternal purpose he has realized in Christ Jesus our Lord.

We receive these riches so that we can have boldness and access with confidence through our faith in him.

God sent Jesus to earth by His grace and working power so that we may receive the unsearchable riches of Christ.

Paul tells us to "therefore, walk boldly and with confidence through your faith in Him (Jesus) because we are partakers of the promise of Christ."[51]

That is a powerful message! You are the partakers of God's promise!

You have been given unsearchable riches of Christ—an unknowable valley of treasures given freely to you. A gift that only God could give with a purpose that only He could fashion.

Remember this:

- The purpose was realized in Christ Jesus.
- The purpose, just like the battle, is already won.
- The purpose is already laid for us, given to the world forever.
- The purpose is finished, it's set, it has been declared, and it comes to pass.
- The purpose has been fulfilled.

The question then becomes, what does that look like in your daily life? That's the fundamental question and reason we struggle: We're not equipped to answer it without living in God's promises. Without the promises, there is no purpose.

Re-Defining Purpose

My purpose in life isn't to be a mom or write a book. Those are things that I do. And as my life shifts, I do different things. Seasons come and go. Chapters begin and end. When I lost a job, I found a new one. When my ministry ended, I found a new place to serve. When my family needed more than I could give, I left the military to care for them. If I find myself bored with my chosen hobbies, I pursue new ones.

Do you see? None of those roles or goals were my purpose. They are simply places and spaces where I uniquely served the world during a specific time and season. They are goals related to my values and passions. And in each of them, I strive to honor God. To live in His promises every single day. I consider what drives and motivates me, but the Great Commandment is at the core of everything I do.

I ask myself these two questions: (1) Does this new thing allow me to love God with my heart, soul, and mind, and (2) does it help me to love my neighbor as myself?

Does it include the three elements of purpose:

1) A Goal (*To Make Disciples*) that has

2) Personal Meaning (*To Bear the Image of Christ*) and is focused

3) Beyond the Self (*For God's Glory*)

If I can answer yes to those three things, my purpose checkbox is selected. Navigating that space daily is more challenging. I focus on God's promises because those elements sustain me and give me hope on discouraging days.

God gave us a perfect plan and set it in motion long before we were born. Trust in His promises, and you will find peace knowing you're living a life of God's divine purpose.

By His Blood

Last year, my brother-in-law passed away. For much of his life, he rejected the grace of God. In conversations, he dismissed His sovereignty. But in his final days, as he lay in his hospital bed, he came face to face with the love of Christ.

While my husband and his brothers prayed for God's mercy upon his body, many came to remember the story of the thief on the cross. It was a staggering reminder of God's promises, regardless of the nature in which we come to meet the Savior.

For many Christians, we can recite the story of the thief on the cross from memory. Jesus went to the unjust trial led by Pontus Pilot and received the sentence of crucifixion.

But He wasn't alone. Two others hung beside Him, one criminal on his left and the other on his right. Jesus said, "Forgive them, Father, for they know not what they do," as the people stood and scoffed at Him. One of the criminals said, "Are you not the Christ? Save yourself and us!" But the other criminal rebuked the first.

He said, "Do not fear God since you are under the sentence of condemnation." We were justly condemned for our sins, but this man (Jesus) is innocent." He said, "Jesus, remember me when you enter your kingdom."

Jesus said, "Truly, I say to you, today you will be with me in paradise" (Luke 23: 26–43).

Let me repeat.

"Today, you will be with me in paradise." There was no 5-step plan. It was only by His word and His blood. The man said, "I believe," therefore, Jesus said, "You are mine."

Unfolding His Promises

We watched that promise unfold with my dear brother, and it was a gentle yet powerful reminder that God's love never ends. His promises remain for each of us.

There was no purpose to my brother's suffering. For those who love him, it was a reminder that God's love can ease the suffering of others. In our weaknesses, we have His strength. In our pain, we carry His hope.

> IN OUR QUEST FOR PURPOSE, WE FIND HIS PROMISES, AND THOSE SUSTAIN US ON DEMANDING DAYS.

In our quest for purpose, we find His promises, and those sustain us on demanding days.

Walking with the Savior

Paulo Coelho enchanted the world with his 1988 novel *The Alchemist,* which tells the story of a shepherd boy named Santiago who launches on a quest to find a hidden treasure. During the story, Santiago travels to faraway lands. He meets many people who offer guidance and direction. But during his quest, his focus shifts from seeking an external treasure to searching for his "personal legend" or purpose. Along the way, Santiago struggles and realizes *the journey is the treasure*. He discovers that "every second of the search is an encounter with God."[1]

Every second of the search is an encounter with God.

Friend, that *is* the point.

As a Christian who spent most of her life wrapped in a blanket of grace, this rings true for me. At its deepest level, our need to define our life's purpose and contain or capitalize on it is our attempt at finding peace. We desire tranquility and wholeness at a deep, demanding level.

I seek a peace within my soul that words or worldly things cannot provide. In this journey with Jesus, I've learned that the quest for purpose is not the answer. The peace came when I discovered God's perfect plan.

His Perfect Plan

Today, I find peace in His loving nature and the sovereignty surrounding me on strenuous days. I find it in the gentle whisper of the morning, the laughter of my children, and the hope that today's suffering will end. I find it in the promise that God will never leave me nor forsake me. Those elements bring peace.

We strive to allow all of God to live through all of us. But we can only do that when we hold onto His promises during every moment of our lives.

In the deepest part of my heart, when I sit and watch the sunrise, golden and flowing over the tall pine trees outside my office window, I ask the Lord, "What is your will today?" And I hear Him say, "You are my beloved, with whom I am well pleased. Tell the world I love her with an everlasting love. That one promise will be with her always.

"Tell her that I see her in all her anxiety and fear. I see her dusty cobwebs wrapped around her banister and the tiredness of her eyes when she crawls into bed after a long day. I see her heart, longing, and suffering. I see her searching for the peace to know that she is loved. And I love her now and forever more."

So, the question is, what does God expect from us?

Quite simply, we are to live in His promises—the gifts and treasures He has given us—every day. And that's not simple. It's not clear or organized. But it's OK. It's OK that it's hard. It's not supposed to be easy.

Does God expect us to try to *discover* our purpose, or should we *rest* in His presence and peace alone?

The answer is the second. And through that rest, the infusion of His spirit and truth through every part of us, we will live fully alive in Him.

Can you imagine it? What would that look like for you? In your daily life? How would it change your church, your community, or your college?

We saw a small glimpse of it at the recent revival at Ashbury University. Students and adults traveled from all over the country to sit at the feet of Jesus. They let the Holy Spirit wash over their broken hearts, tattered bodies, and bruised souls. We watched the power of redemption as people drew closer to the Savior.

That, my friend, is what a promise looks like. And in that promise, there is a divine, holy purpose.

A Prayer for the One Seeking God's Plan for their Life

Dear Lord,

Today, I pray to seek Your perfect plan above my own. May Your grace wrap around me with warmth and protection on difficult days. Allow me to remember how Your sovereignty reigns above all else. In each trial, may I find Your light hidden in the darkest places of my life, and may I always remember that You love me forevermore.

Amen.

THE PROMISES OF GOD

Blessed is she who has believed that
the Lord would fulfill his promises to her!

—*Luke 1:45*

In the 2nd grade, I had a best friend. We spent weekends together running around our farms. Mine sat on a few acres outside of our small oilfield town, and hers lay in the opposite direction. She raised pigs, and we corralled cows. Together, we climbed fences and crawled across hay bales stacked in the old tin barn behind my house. We shared sleepovers and scampered across the balance beams at recess.

But as time passed, we grew distant. In middle school, we made new friends and barely spoke outside the classroom. By the time we made it to high school, we never spent time together. Now, in our mid-40s, we offer an occasional smiley face or heart emoji on Facebook, but other than that, our lives drifted apart 30 years ago. But when we were little, I remember saying, "I promise to be your best friend forever." Unfortunately, that promise didn't last.

Promises are essential. They form the bonds of trust in our most precious relationships. Like nothing else, a promise is a commitment to fulfill a solemn vow. Unfortunately, humans often fail to keep them. But not God. God *never* breaks His promises.

The Certainty of God

In Hebrews, we are reminded of the certainty of God's promises.

> *"For when God made a promise to Abraham since he had no one greater by whom to swear, he swore by himself, saying, "Surely, I will bless you and multiply you. And thus Abraham, having patiently waited, obtained the promise."*

The writer continues to tell us about the character of God, His promise, and His purpose.

> *"When God desired to show more convincingly to the heirs of the promise the unchangeable character of his purpose, he guaranteed it with an oath."*[52]

The word purpose is translated in Greek as *boules*,[53] which means the unchangeableness of His purpose or the counsel of Him that He *guaranteed*. We find it used 12 times in the New Testament.

In Acts 4:28, 13:36, and 20:27, the same word references God's purposes or counsel. These Scriptures remind us that God's promises are unchangeable, just like His purpose. God made promises to His chosen people. God is faithful.

The Faithfulness of God

One of my favorite stories in the Bible is about the Israelites wandering in the wilderness for 40 years. What fascinates me is not their wandering specifically but how they lived each day. What did their daily lives look like as they tried to raise their families, protect their flocks, and continue to learn how to trust in God's sovereignty?

One of the most transformative lessons is how they followed the cloud. In Exodus 13:21–22, Scripture tells us, *"And the Lord went before them by day in a pillar of a cloud, to lead them the way, and by night in a pillar of fire, to give them light."*

Can you imagine it?

We're sitting at the base of Mount Sinai, watching a cloud move across the landscape.

A cloud. A simple cloud.

I have so many questions.

- How big was it?
- Was there a "cloud watcher" assigned to yell to the rest of the group when it started to move?
- If so, were they responsible for gathering the tribes and saying, "OK, the cloud is moving, so let's pack up and go"?
- Or was it less rapid and more predictable?
- How fast did the cloud move?
- Did it change colors from white to gray to black?

See, I have so many questions.

But I imagine it was a slow process for the Israelites. I'm speculating at best, but it always fascinates me how they could just follow a cloud. How could they do that?

In my walk with the Lord, I try to focus on "the cloud," learning to lean into the Spirit to discern if God is moving so I can be ready.

It is faith, this I know, but it's complicated. I find solace in the fact that it's not just the Christians of today who struggle to discern the hand or plans of God.

Remember, God gave the covenant to Abraham. In the story of Genesis, God told Abraham that he would become the leader among many nations. God promised to give him descendants as numerous as the stars in the sky.[54]

That promise, called the *Abrahamic Covenant*, included four essential elements: land, descendants, a covenant relationship with God, and a blessing to the nations. But that promise took years to fulfill. It would be another 645 years[55] between the time God called Abraham and the Israelites left Egypt with Moses.

How could a nation that never heard the promise sustain its focus for 645 years? They believed in God's promises, yes, but they lived by faith and hope.

A Life of Faith

In Romans 4:13–15, Paul tells us that the promise God gave to Abraham and his children was not offered because of something that Abraham did or would do in the future. It was based on God's decision to provide it through the *righteousness of faith*. I love how the Message version of the Bible explains it:

> *"If those who get what God gives them only get it by doing everything they are told to do and filling out all the right forms properly signed, that eliminates personal trust. It turns the promise into an ironclad contract! That's not a holy promise; that's a business deal."*[56]

This is why the fulfillment of God's promise depends entirely on trusting God *and his way and then simply embracing him and what he does.* God's promise arrives as a pure gift. *That's the only way everyone can be sure to get in on it: those who keep the religious traditions and those who have never heard of them.*[57]

If the promise is only for those who obey the laws, then the promise is void. That's why it depends on faith. Every promise rests on grace and is guaranteed to all of Abraham's offspring, not only to those who follow the law but to those who share in the faith of Abraham.

Hebrews reminds us, "We have a sure and steadfast anchor of the soul, a hope that enters into the inner palace behind the curtain, where Jesus has gone as a forerunner on our behalf."[58]

God made the covenant with Abraham and his descendants for eternity. But our new covenant was found in the life, death, and resurrection of Jesus Christ.

The Power to Transform Lives

For 13 years, I've served in the crisis pregnancy help ministry. In 2018, after evaluating our ministry and the community's needs, we created a 501(c)3 nonprofit organization. I still remember the night our senior pastor printed out the IRS 1023 form in his tiny office.

We sat discussing how we could bring the monstrous vision to life. At the end, he handed me the form and said, "Danita, you'll have to become a nonprofit." I reached up and nervously took the form.

I had no idea what that meant or what it would entail. I simply believed God had given us a vision for our community. To help the hurting, we needed more. That was my only frame of reference.

My next steps weren't driven by purpose or destiny or even calling. They manifested as my story unfolded into a tapestry of moments, walking with God through unfamiliar seasons. We didn't have a 5-point plan. We simply followed "the cloud" God set before us each week. As one task closed, another appeared. As one person left, another came to take their place. Still today, God continues to bring hurting people into my path. In each encounter, I strive to see God's hand stretched out before us.

But our journey was never about purpose, or at least not mine. We still struggle to see the path. We still spend countless hours in prayer, searching for a glimpse of the Lord's hand at work.

We still don't have a 5-step plan, but we have the promises of God. And we strive to live in them each and every day.

Living a Life of Promise

So, what does a life of promise look like? Romans tells us that when we rejoice in our suffering, specific things happen:

- Suffering produces endurance
- Endurance produces character
- Character produces hope[59]

Hope does not put us to shame because God's love has been poured into our hearts through the Holy Spirit, who has been given to us (Romans 5:3–5).

When I think about living a life of promise, I liken it to dancing on a teeter-totter or navigating a tightrope walk across Niagara Falls.

But rest assured, it isn't. The God of the universe, who calls you and keeps you, understands everything. As 2 Corinthians 5:7 says, "For we walk by faith, not by sight."

That's complicated. What is it like to walk by faith? To have eyes to see what is unseeable. To have ears to hear what others cannot hear.

I don't know what that looks like for you. For me, it's like being in a dark room. I'm sometimes only inching toward the Savior one step at a time. In those moments, I often hear the same simple question I heard years ago: "What do you have in your hand today, Danita? Use that one thing. That's all I asked you to do today."

In that moment, I focus, for as much as my human mind can muster, on looking for His promises.

Discovering God's Promises

In Psalm 119, the psalmist examines God's promises. But before we look at the promises, remember one crucial element: God gives us guideposts along our purpose journey.

The brightest one is His Word. "God's word is a lamp for my feet and a light on my path" (Psalm 119:105). We use God's Word as our guidepost. Without it, we are lost at sea, floating in the darkness for literal eternity.

You can't find God's promises without His Word. And in God's Word, we find His promises laid out before us like gifts waiting to be both received and revealed:

- The Lord will fulfill His promises to those who fear him (v38).

- The Lord will bring comfort in times of suffering (v50).

- His unfailing love will come to you (v41.)

- He will be gracious to you (v58).

- He will sustain you (v116).

- He will defend your cause and redeem you (v154).

- He will deliver you from your petitions and requests (v170).

- His promises are thoroughly tested (v140).

- Despite when our eyes fail, his promises remain (v123).

Do you see, friend? We may not be able to find the answers to the next ten years or ten minutes of our lives, but we can commit ourselves to following the Lord and focusing daily on His promises.

Say, "Lord, I will follow you. I will take up my cross daily and seek to share your love with the world." That is what living each day in God's promises and divine purpose looks like. In Part 3 of this book, we'll dig into those promises and discover what it's like to live a life of promise over purpose. But remember that God's promises are the air that we breathe. Without them, nothing else matters.

The Breath of God

His promises are for all of us. Not for our acts but only through grace and faith. Did you catch that? Faith believes in what cannot be seen. Grace receives that which can never be earned.

In both elements, we see how the gift of life and breath on this earth have nothing to do with our actions. It has everything to do with God's undeniable, unquenchable breath—the *ruak*—as it moves through us. And if we are to live in the promises of God, then we must first begin to understand that faith, like breath, is often hard to see.

You can't see your breath if you're sitting on the beach on a sunny afternoon or at your desk at work. But it's there. It's the life force and sustaining factor you need for everything. God's promises are like that. Sustaining elements. We need them even though we can't always see them. Purpose seems fickle but promises are faithful.

Forevermore

God offers promises that we can cling to amid challenging times. We have His promises when we see that our pursuit of purpose might be less about eternity and more about the here and now. In Jeremiah 31:3, the Lord tells Israel, "I have loved you with an everlasting love."

God's promises reassure us when hope, faith, or purpose disappear. A.W. Tozer reminds us that "God's oath and covenant

GOD'S PROMISES REASSURE US WHEN HOPE, FAITH, OR PURPOSE DISAPPEAR.

secured the promised land. All the infinite resources of God are behind the covenant. God delivers His promises because He is God."[60]

One of the greatest promises is that God will remember our sins no more: "For I will be merciful toward their iniquities and remember their sins no more" (Hebrews 8:12).

That, dear friend, should give us the greatest peace: realizing that God promises to grant us mercy and to forget our sins no more. That promise contains eternal hope. And in the hope, we find the comfort and peace to know that despite the pain of today, we stand firm in God's promises forever.

Embracing the Promise

For five years, my sacred friend, April, batted metastatic breast cancer. Cancer ravaged her body, destroyed her dreams and hopes for her future. I watched in distant dismay, as she and her family endured this crippling disease. Day after day, they clung to grace like a handrail; it was their lifeline.

One day, she and I sat and talked about me writing a book. I am sure we talked about other things as well. Our conversations often flowed between random topics, as friendships often do. But at one point, she said, "Danita, what's the point? What if you write one book, or two or three? What then? What's next? What will you do when you reach the end and nothing is left?"

I sat with a heaviness in my chest as I realized what she was asking. I said, "Well, I'll probably sit on my porch and cry. And then, I'll wipe my face and start anew."

She nodded.

The lesson for me was simple yet profound.

If we spend our lives chasing after purpose, what happens when we "get there"? Better yet, what happens when we don't?

Watching April battle cancer changed my perspective. While I never wanted to carry the weight of her diagnosis, I

> IF WE SPEND OUR LIVES CHASING AFTER PURPOSE, WHAT HAPPENS WHEN WE "GET THERE"? BETTER YET, WHAT HAPPENS WHEN WE DON'T?

saw it change her view of her world, her faith, and her purpose. The lenses she looked through were different than mine. The difference in our perspectives was more evident because she faced the finality and frailty of life—those challenges I have not yet faced.

So, I offer this last question to you, friend: what lens will you use to look at the world?

Will you choose the lens that society offers? Or will you put down your purpose glasses and pick up a new set of lenses? The ones that see the world through God's eyes? The ones that see that you're surrounded by gifts and blessings that God has laid out before you every single moment of every single day?

The choice is yours.

A Place of Refuge

My home is in the Uwharrie National Forest, insulated between hundreds of acres of longleaf and loblolly pine trees that tower above us like soldiers guarding a fortress. Their purpose is vast:

to provide oxygen, fuel, or warmth and to be made into beautiful things like tables, lamps, or homes. We search for the depth of their beauty and design. At first glance, a tree is just a tree. But inside, it contains every essence it was created to hold.

We don't make trees or manufacture their beauty in man-made places. Each one is unique and beautifully designed. Intimate. Hand-selected. Beautiful in its time. When you look inside it, past the bark and the leaves, you see an intricate design consisting of patterns, rings, and sap edges that tell a beautiful story of how it was formed. All the elements of the world combine to create it—heat, rain, humidity, insects, or parasites burrow deep inside its soft bark. And in that story, we see beauty.

We see strength.

We see a majestic oak that towers above the rest, holding out its branches for safety and comfort.

Those are God's promises, friend.

They are constant, never changing, and eternal.

God's promises must be universal for the equation to remain true. The promise must be equally available for the mother and the childless alike. It must be true for the daughter and the orphan. It must be true for the cancer survivor and the one lying in the hospital bed. It must be true for all, or the gospel algorithm is false.

I choose to set my eyes upon the promises of God. To allow their peace to sustain me as I walk through life with my Savior, hand in hand, on hard days and glorious ones. Together. We go together.

I invite you, friend, to do the same. To lay down your pursuit of purpose so that you can find rest in the arms and promises of a sovereign, holy God who loves you without blame or blemish.

The time is now. I offer this prayer to you, the one who has navigated the purpose journey and sits now at the sacred place where God's promises are revealed.

A Prayer to See God's Promises

Dear Lord,

May the hope and love that only You can give wash over me today. Let me choose to put on new lenses to see Your promises in all things, both the good and the hard. As Your Word says, may You always light my path and draw me close to You. And when I stumble, shine a light onto my feet so I can walk each day with You.

Amen.

PART I REFLECTION:

UNWRAPPING YOUR PURPOSE PARADOX

UNWRAPPING YOUR PURPOSE PARADOX

Guideposts and Reflection

Often, we don't have a chance to explore our purpose questions. This space allows you to examine the previous chapters to help you replace your pursuit of purpose with walking daily in God's promises.

Chapter 1: Quest for Purpose

1) Now that we've studied the definition of purpose, what changed about your understanding or perception of asking, "What is my purpose?"

_____

_____

_____

_____

_____

_____

_____

Chapter 2: The Anxiety of Purpose

2) In the "Actual Self" column, write down five traits that describe how you are. In the "Ideal Self" column, write down five traits describing the person you think you ought to be. (Example: Actual Self: *I'm impatient* Ideal Self: *I need more patience.*)

Actual Self	Ideal Self
1. _____	a) _____
2. _____	b) _____
3. _____	c) _____
4. _____	d) _____
5. _____	e) _____

3) How do those traits differ?

_____

_____

_____

4) How do they affect your perception of your identity and purpose?

_____

_____

_____

Chapter 3: God's Perfect Plan

5) What foundational promises keep you grounded when everything else disappears?

_____

_____

_____

6) How can you focus on the promises of God instead of being fixed on your life's purpose?

_____

_____

_____

Chapter 4: The Promises of God

The psalmist gives many examples of God's promises in the following passages.

- 38 - Fulfill your promise to your servant so that you may be feared.
- 41 - May your unfailing love come to me according to your promise.
- 50 - My comfort in my suffering is this: Your promise preserves my life.

- 58 - I have sought your face with all my heart; be gracious according to your promise.

- 116 - Sustain me, according to your promise; do not let my hopes be dashed.

- 123 - My eyes fail, looking for your salvation and righteous promise.

- 140 - Your promises have been thoroughly tested, and your servant loves them.

- 154 - Defend my cause and redeem me; preserve my life according to your promise.

- 170 - May my supplication come before you; deliver me according to your promise.

7) Which of these promises have you incorporated into your daily life?

_____

_____

_____

8) Which promise has never or rarely been considered in your life?

_____

_____

_____

9) How can you shift your focus daily to see His promises more clearly?

_____

_____

_____

Journal

To the one struggling today to make sense of your purpose, I offer this gift to you. This is a place to lay down your fears and anxiety and let the God of the universe, the One who fashioned you by unique design and called you by name, bring peace into your life. Use this space to lay down what you no longer wish to carry about your purpose.

_____

_____

_____

_____

_____

_____

_____

_____

_____

A Prayer for You

Dear Lord,

Today, I offer my heart into Your sovereign hands. The heart that wants, with desperation, to know that I am living a life fully dedicated to Your purpose and plan. Please give me the clarity and wisdom to see when my pursuit of purpose pulls me away from You. Replace that pursuit with Your promises so I can commune with You each moment. Thank You for the abundance of blessings You have provided. Let me continue this journey, walking hand in hand with You.

Amen.

PART II: THE IDOL OF PURPOSE

REDISCOVER YOUR IDENTITY IN CHRIST

My identity is defined by a mighty Savior unseen.

—Cali Willette, *Fractures of Gold*

I grew up in the oilfields of Oklahoma, where, as the famous Rodgers and Hammerstein song says, the wind goes "sweeping down the plains."

And it does. It really does.

As a young girl, I watched the long, emerald stocks of wheat dance as the wind stirred across the open plains. In the Midwest, the wind never stops. It blasts the bystander with the bitter, relentless cold of a winter day or the scorching heat of a dry summer afternoon. Now that I'm older, I no longer live in the Midwest. But I often remember the wind.

Growing up in that oilfield town, my family struggled. My parents didn't always get along, and we spent nights at the sheriff's station or hiding inside an undisclosed women's shelter, seeking refuge from the latest storm.

During those times, I learned that the winds of life often burst across our lives without care for our senses or protection. When they do, we are left holding on to whatever we can grasp until the storms cease or until we topple over, whatever comes first.

We conjoin thousands of memories and moments of our lives into the tapestry we call "identity." Sometimes, we allow the hardest parts to creep into the purest places of our hearts and souls. We wield them as the shield for our broken, battered bodies. We search for our worth in their promises, but those promises never come true.

The purpose pendulum swings between various points in our lives. Some struggle to find answers to their purpose questions because they focus on the pain of their past. Others may question their purpose despite having lived in trauma or pain. They may have lived a "good life" and struggled to see their purpose. It's challenging to see God's hand in their lives because, simply put, they're fine.

Regardless of where you sit on the purpose + identity pathway, we all struggle to understand our identity in Christ.

Finding Your Identity in Christ

Scripture teaches that we become a new creation when we surrender our lives to follow Christ.

Our identity rests in Him alone.

Paul reminds us, *"Therefore, if anyone is in Christ, the new creation has come; the old is gone, the new is here!"*[61] This is the most important element in understanding how to live a life of divine purpose and focus on God's promises: You must first find your identity *in Christ.*

We know that, but it's tougher than we realize. When we look to the Scriptures for guidance on overcoming an identity crisis, no other person carried the mantle greater than Joseph.

The Great Identity Crisis

Joseph, the youngest brother of 12, lived a life as his father's favorite child. God began to send him dreams at a young age. He would proclaim the dreams to his father and brothers, often with a tinge of arrogance attached. It was probably a symptom of his youth. But over time, his brothers became angry with him. One day, their jealousy got the best of them.

They took Joseph and planned to kill him. But at the last minute, his brother Reuben intervened, and they threw him in a well. As a band of travelers moved across the desert, they bargained to sell him into captivity.

So, here is Joseph. In one day, he went from being the beloved son of Jacob to a slave, forgotten and condemned by his brothers—those who were supposed to love and protect him.

Joseph travels across the land and has many experiences along the way. But God is always with him.

Years after he served Pharaoh, spent time in prison, and refused sexual advances, God placed him in a position equal to his identity.

Of course, Jesus was not born yet, and Joseph doesn't know how the Messiah will come, be sacrificed and resurrected. But he finds his purpose in God's promises. All along the way, Joseph clings to the promises of God.

Joseph learns to forgive despite his circumstances. We can understand his desire to carry regret, shame, or disappointment. But instead, he serves. He prays. He honors God in all things. And in the crucible of obedience, God upholds His promises. In the end, God allows Joseph to take care of not only his family but also the nations of Egypt during the famine. He moves his family into a new land and sets them up for future generations.

Sold Into Slavery

Most of us have never been sold into slavery by those we love. But you don't have to be someone who suffered trauma or abuse to struggle to find your identity in Christ. We all struggle with defining our identity at different times and across varying degrees. Knowing your true self in Christ requires you to experience love in a vulnerable way.

Consider the first time you saw Jesus' face. Remember that moment when you saw His love and understood, for as much as your human heart could endure, the grace that came from His sovereign sacrifice.

In that space, you experienced the vulnerability of a "just as I am" encounter.[62] You came face to face with the Messiah and let His love pour over you. At times, that kind of love is distressing to receive. For us to truly receive it, we must be undefended. Our guard and defenses must be lowered to let the love of Christ shine into our darkest spaces.

That shining of His light allows us to rediscover our identity in Him *alone*.

We see how our purpose is to love Him and to love the world.

> **WE SEE HOW OUR PURPOSE IS TO LOVE HIM AND TO LOVE THE WORLD.**

And through that light, we discover His promises.

Too often, we try to ride on a pendulum that swings between our belief

94

in scarcity and reliance upon self-sufficiency, leaving us confused and isolated. We struggle to lay down our defenses and see that our need for purpose and peace comes from a greater place driven by our response to either grief or fear. Both cause great deception when considering our pursuit of purpose and our identity in Christ.

The Deception of Scarcity

Have you driven through a tunnel in the mountains? Growing up in the Midwest, we didn't often navigate through mountains or tunnels. But after moving to North Carolina, I've spent many hours traveling across the Appalachian Mountains. At first, the mountains and tunnels were overwhelming. But as I've grown accustomed to them, I'm less anxious on our yearly drives to see family.

The tunnel is designed with a purpose. It is reinforced to hold back the power and weight of the mountain, giving the commuters a direct path from one point to the next. They are engineering feats. Nothing gets past the barrier of a tunnel. If it does, then we have problems! As our car enters its circular space, our eyes shift. As we drive through them, we can only see the tunnel. Everything outside the tunnel is foggy. Depending upon the size or length of it, we may not even be able to see the end. We can only focus on the sharp images of cars or headlights in front of us.

This is how scarcity works. In scarcity, we focus on one thing. We tend to focus on that which needs to be included. As the proverbial quote says, "We can't see the forest for the trees."

But scarcity often leads to dissatisfaction and struggle. Scarcity is a mindset, a choice. We have a subjective perception of what matters in our lives.[63] Often, we only focus on the darkness when we try to find the purpose in our pain. Scarcity makes us believe that something is missing and there is a gap or void that we need to fill. And we become so hyper-focused on that gap that nothing else matters. We believe the lie that tells us we are not worthy of God's love. We become isolated and lose hope.

Often, scarcity is a response to the need to grieve. Loss, pain, and suffering are real. But isolation keeps us from finding God's promises in our lives. It's not a new tactic in the spiritual world. We first see it at the beginning of the Scriptures when Eve is walking in the Garden of Eden.

In Genesis 3:1, we are introduced to the serpent. And he says, "Did God say, 'You were not to eat from any tree in the garden'?"[64] And here the deception begins.

But notice that Satan waited until Eve was alone. He waited until she was walking alone to deceive her mind. He slowly reached into her heart and started to tear down the bridge of trust she had formed with God.

She trusted God.

She *knew* Him.

She walked with him in the garden and shared intimacy with him.

But now, Satan is telling her that God may have lied. Maybe the God she trusts is not 100% honest with her. She starts to pull away from the peace and security she had and finds herself alone.

Isolation can be our greatest enemy when we search for answers to our purpose questions. In that struggle, we tell ourselves we are not worthy of God's love. We assume His promise is for someone else. If the world knew about our past failures, abuse, or painful stories, they would know we don't deserve to sit at God's holy table.

We may even believe we will always be or feel broken, shattered, isolated, unseen, or unworthy. We may never shake the dark cloud that looms over us. In those moments, we ask, "How are we supposed to find purpose in this pain? How are we supposed to look forward and see God's promises when all we can see is this messy thing?"

Dear friend, you are not what the world says about you. You are not what has been done to you or what you failed to do. You are worth more than diamonds or gold. But it's often baffling to believe this when life has hurt you.

We must learn to trust in God's promises no matter what trials life throws at our feet.

Pain or disappointment can make us feel isolated from the world. The same is true if we look at our life and see a combination of average, nothing special, everyday moments. In this space, we become apathetic to the world around us. We consider the sufficiency of our lives and miss out on the personal intimacy and divine encounter with a holy, sovereign God.

The Deceit of Self-Sufficiency

But what do you do when your life is relatively safe and warm? You grew up with a safe, loving family, had an enjoyable childhood, and launched into the world with certainty and focus. Maybe you've had a successful career and navigated your vocational ladder with confidence and success.

Over the years, I've worked with pastors, youth ministers, teachers, military leaders, and parents who grew up in loving and nurturing homes. Their parents taught them about the love of Christ, and as far back as they can remember, they've always believed in God. They have successful careers, love their families well, and are confident in their faith. But in that, they also struggle to see God's promises. At times, they've become apathetic to them. They have a "good" life and find comfort in their resources, security, and past accomplishments. But this is not what living a life of divine promise looks like.

Just like Peter, we're invited to step out of the security of our "lifeboat" and take hold of the sovereign God. Jesus calls us to vulnerability, not self-sufficiency. He meets us in our suffering and our apathy alike. He offers us another perspective: Love me and love the world.

At times, we find ourselves comfortable with Christ. We live under the blanket of our self-sufficient strength, which keeps us from finding God's peace and provision.

When we take the steps toward the Savior, we find newness within our hearts, souls, minds, and strength. Our identity is rooted and established in His eternal love.

Rooted In Love

In the Bible, we read how God is always a God of love. The beloved John teaches us to *love because God first loved us.*[65] Despite our pain, anxiety, grief, or fear, we can, without fail, reach back into these sovereign Scriptures and discover, repeatedly, how much God loves us.

Sometimes, when we've lived a hardship, we struggle to see how it can be used for "God's glory." We ask, "What is the purpose of my pain?" Unfortunately, that question clouds our perspective. It changes our focus. And in those moments, we draw our eyes away from Him and onto ourselves.

Over the years, I've learned the thing that causes me the greatest pain can be a catalyst for change. It's as if God is waiting to reach inside and take hold of what hurts so He can say, "Now, give that to me. I will use this for my glory."

Despite the pain of my past or my tarnished identity perspective, I learned that God's promises are true. But that, friend, requires trust. Trust is a difficult thing to find. For those of us who've been hurt by this world, by those we trusted, or by those we loved, it's even harder.

For me, growing up in that little oilfield town was grinding. Our family faced many storms. But despite them, we always knew that our parents loved us, no matter what. That foundational truth carried me through many difficult times. It carried me through the questions that ensued as I tried to learn how to reconcile my version of love with the love of my Savior. It carried me through divorce, disease, and depression.

It can be difficult to reconcile our purpose or identity with the promise of God's love. But God did not design us for confusion. God is a God of love—always. In His arms, there is protection. In His shelter, there is peace. In Psalm 5:11–12 (NIV), the psalmist reassures us that God protects us:

But let all who take refuge in you be glad; let them ever sing for joy. Spread your protection over them so those who love your name may rejoice in you. Surely, Lord, you bless the righteous; you surround them with your favor as with a shield.

We must respond with a humble heart. As Saint Augustine of Hippo explains, the more we learn about ourselves, the more we can know God.[66] The basis for our identity is found in Jesus Christ.

Our identity comprises several things. By leaning into the verse in Mark 12:30, *"And you shall love the Lord your God with all your heart and with all your soul and with all your mind and with all your strength,"* we find the tools to rediscover our identity in Christ.

Those four elements create the steps to enter the deep pool with Christ.

Repair Your Heart

In her book *Learning to Walk in the Dark*, Barbara Brown Taylor explores the concept of physical and emotional darkness. She spent many years as an Episcopal priest, serving as the on-call chaplain at the local hospital in Atlanta. During her evening shifts, she stood with families as they lost loved ones.

She shares her fear and emotions as she walked each night into hospital rooms with a Bible instead of a stethoscope to offer solace during the hardest moments.

She learned that "nights like those taught me the importance of letting emotions flow—even the loud and messy ones—because if they are kept from making their noise, they can clot like plaque in a coronary artery, blocking anything else that tries to come through."[67]

I experienced that same thing during my grieving years. It was as if a roaring ocean of pain waited to cascade over my life. No matter what I did or how much I tried to outrun it, the wave moved ever closer. In the end, I could do nothing except let the feelings flow.

My only sustaining power was the love of Christ. I clung to the promise in 1 Corinthians 13:4–8, which reminds us:

> Love is patient and kind; love does not envy or boast; it is not arrogant or rude. It does not insist on its way; it is not irritable or resentful; it does not rejoice at wrongdoing but rejoices with the truth. Love bears all things, believes all things, hopes all things, and endures all things. Love never ends.

Sometimes, the love of an earthly father can be complicated. Those experiences make it troublesome to trust a holy Father unlike any you've ever known.

As you work to rediscover your identity in Christ, you must take time to repair your heart. At times, the world applies pain without approval. It takes time and intention to remove those layers and replace them with the vision and divine purpose that only God provides.

Renew Your Mind

When we consider our identity, we must also change our thoughts. Thoughts are like clouds. They come and go, but we choose which thoughts to believe and which to act upon.

Take, for instance, my love of cupcakes. I love them. Truly. Like coffee, cupcakes are a gift from heaven. And I would like to have one every single day. But if I act on those thoughts, I will feel sluggish, and my pants will soon burst at the seams!

It's a simple example, but the premise is important. When we consider our pursuit of purpose, our thoughts influence our beliefs, which in turn shape our identity. Our perceived identity influences our behaviors. Proverbs says, "For as a man thinketh within himself, so is he."[68]

You are what you think.

In today's culture, we see a lot of information about positive thinking and the power of visualization. Sometimes, the concept receives criticism, but the premise is important because belief influences both our and other people's behaviors.

When you see your identity and divine purpose in Christ, you can reframe your perspectives about your past, present, and future. When you choose to focus on God's promises, you start to see them in all things—both the grim and the good. And in those moments, we find our minds shift. Our negative thoughts or fears begin to pass away when we see and know we have hope in Christ.

We begin to see God's promises in all things as they surround and envelop us. The infusion of His love changes the way we think.

Rest Your Soul

Like the making of constellations, I wonder about the soul. Where does it come from? Where does it go? Have you wondered as well?

C.S. Lewis explains that "the soul is but a hollow which God fills."[69] In this example, the soul seems like a vast and infinite vessel, like space. We imagine that if God is omnipresent, in and above all things, and fills the soul, then isn't it also infinite?

Counselor and author John Eldredge reminds us, "I know the soul isn't a shallow puddle. It's deep and vast, capable of symphonies and heroic courage. But it is finite. It was never designed to carry the sorrows of this world."[70]

Our souls are finite. They have limitations. Only God is infinite. Therefore, as Jesus teaches us in Matthew, we learn to place our care and burdens upon the Lord. *Take my yoke upon you, and learn from me, for I am gentle and lowly in heart, and you will find rest for your souls.*[71]

Like our physical bodies, hearts, and minds, our souls need rest. Seeing God's promises is difficult when you're filled with the world's sorrows. Purpose becomes confusing, frustrating, and overwhelming. It's like a garden hose with a kink in the middle. As much as you pull and squeeze, the water cannot reach the end of the nozzle.

If we are to truly live in God's peace and promises, we must make a space for our souls to rest.

But how do we make a space that allows more of God and less of the world into our souls? John reminds us, "Your soul is the vessel God fills, yet there is no room for him to fill if your soul is wrung out, twisted, haggard, fried."[72]

For God to fill your soul, you must make space for Him to dwell. That starts with laying life at His feet and asking God to replace your pursuit of purpose with His promises.

Replenish Your Strength

For almost 30 years, I served alongside the U.S. military. America's heroes and legends are what I like to call them. Not me. I'm just a girl who is good with Excel spreadsheets. But for a season, I had the humble pleasure of sitting at the table with those we consider the strongest warriors.

In that season, I learned that strength is not what we think it is. True strength comes in the quiet. It comes in the stillness before the storm. Strength and courage are not always actions. At times, they are waiting. When we rest and wait for the whisper of God to move in our lives, we find strength.

When we consider our identity as it relates to purpose, we must replenish our strength in the Lord. The world tells us that strength is different. It's loud and boastful. Like leadership, we confuse strength with power.

But loving the Lord our God with all our strength comes from a deeper place of surrender. I understand the paradox between surrender and strength. *"In returning and rest, you shall be saved; in quietness and trust shall be your strength"* (Isaiah 30:15).

Imagine God standing before you today with His arms and power stretched out like a shield, enveloping you with His words, strength, promises, and provision. As a child of Christ, you are called to love God with your heart, mind, soul, and strength. That's draining when your heart is worn, your soul is weary, your mind wanders, and your strength wavers.

But here is the key: **Finding the peace *of* Christ requires you to place your identity *in* Christ.**

You are a new creation who must learn daily to rely on God's promises.

We do that by walking together with the Savior.

Walking with the Savior

As a child, I was never baptized. I gave my life to the Lord on a little white church bus in my hometown when I was nine. But then, my life was less than holy or faithful as I navigated a path of youth and emotional pain. Years later, after encountering Jesus, I turned my face toward him and tried to refocus my life.

When our small church in Oklahoma offered baptism, my husband and I signed up. Each week, we attended church and met with a small group of friends who helped us learn to walk with God. We spent hours discussing the love of Christ, studying Scripture, drinking coffee, and eating snacks as our 12 children ran around the house, making friends and fighting dragons in the back bedroom.

This small group of friends became our spiritual lifeline. I struggled to walk with Jesus in my early days, but they were always there to pick us up, no matter how many times we fell.

The Friday night before my baptism, I was undone. I wrestled with the pain and shame of my past, convinced that I was not worthy of baptism. I was not worthy of God's love because of my past choices. Each memory crashed over me like a wave, knocking against my heart and mind so violently that I was convinced it would be best to maintain my current life. But despite the shame I felt, I desperately wanted God's love.

During our small group that night, one dear friend sat with me on my couch as our kids ran through the house with plastic swords and cups filled with Doritos. I shared my confusion with her. She said, "Salvation is not about being worthy. It's about grace. Paul murdered Christians, and God used him. So, if God can redeem a murderer, think about how much he loves you, too." I smiled through tears but still found my identity in my past mistakes.

On Sunday, I wept. I cried as I dressed for church, drove to the service, and stood behind the curtain, waiting for my baptism. I sobbed in the silence, hoping no one would hear me. But as I stepped into the makeshift pool, filled with warm water, I took my husband's hand and looked at our pastor. He smiled at me with the knowing look of a fellow warrior who navigated a rugged road. Then he turned to our congregation and said, "Sometimes, the power of God's grace is overwhelming." I nodded through my tears.

As my husband laid me beneath the water and pulled me back to the surface, I knew that moment was the beginning of something new.

It wasn't an easy or fast journey. There have been many disorienting days. But when I look back at my life, faults, or failures, I remember that I was made new—in Him.

And the promise that He has loved me with an everlasting love carries me.

It gives me strength.

It gives me hope.

It silences the voices that tell me I am not worthy.

It points me back to His arms, always.

And in that voice, I find the peace to know that I am walking in the promises and purpose of God despite the difficulties I face.

When I had nothing left to cling to, I found God's love. For the first time, I saw that neither my past nor my purpose defined me.

My identity is, and will always be, rooted in one foundational promise: God's amazing love.

Friend, your identity is in Christ alone. Allow His promises to renew you today: heart, mind, soul, and strength, so you can enjoy the peace of walking in His amazing love.

A Prayer for Renewing Your Identity in Christ

Dear Lord,

Remind me today that my identity is found in You alone. Let the years of false promises wash away from my heart. Replace them with Your sovereign promises so I can see and know that I am Your chosen one. Let me discover the deception of identity daily, and when those things creep into my heart and mind, give me strength and confidence to remain steadfast in You.

Amen.

WHEN PURPOSE BECOMES PERFORMANCE

Man's mind plans his way, but the Lord directs his steps.

—Proverbs 16:9

Most of us have a daily routine. We get up, make coffee, feed the cats, and take the kids to school. Then we go to work where we spend 8 to 12 hours pouring out the best of ourselves into the world.

After a long day, we leave that place and return to our homes and families. We make dinner, feed the cats, and get ready for bed. If we're lucky, we fall into a peaceful slumber, and tomorrow, the cycle continues.

Rinse and repeat.

Humans spend an enormous amount of time wandering the world, trying to decide what to do with their lives. Gettysburg College determined the average person spends 90,000 hours at work.[73] We may be accountants, teachers, warriors, or medical professionals. We own small businesses, work in cubicles, drive trucks, or serve in full-time ministry. Despite how we spend our days, our vocations influence our purpose journey. It consumes most of our life, time, focus, finances, and energy. We assume it is the primary vehicle to fulfill or find our "life's purpose."

But is it?

If we revisit the Great Commandment discussed in Chapter 1, we see how Jesus told us to love Him and the world. Our vocation can impact our ability to comply. Outside of our family, vocation is the largest branch on which we offer our fruits to the world. As Jesus reminds us in John 15:5, "I am the vine, and you are the branches. If you remain in me and I in you, you will bear much fruit; apart from me, you can do nothing."

Our accomplishments may hinder our ability to overcome the idol of purpose. Like identity, performance fuels actions at a deep, often unexplored level of our psyche. We must dive below the water's surface to see the elements of our performance iceberg. But first, let's uncover the purpose of work.

The Purpose of Work

Rev. Dr. Mark D. Roberts[74] is a senior strategist, pastor, author, and speaker. As the Executive Director of the Max De Pree Center for Leadership, he focuses on spiritual development and thriving. In his blog, he shares how Christians traditionally think of work as a way of "embodying our faith."[75] Dr. Roberts instructs us to "Give ourselves fully to the work of the Lord because the Lord is already fully at work in us."[76]

Before the fall, God gave us meaningful work. Embodying our faith through our works is both complicated and beautiful. At times, we see it as a burden and a blessing. Humans need food, clothing, shelter, and safety to survive. But the motivation behind why or how we get them can be misunderstood.

The Hierarchy of Needs

Human needs follow a hierarchy, which Abraham Maslow coined to explain how people seek to meet their psychological and physical needs. In his 1943 paper, "A Theory of Human Motivation," he offered the world a human development system that explained a universal need of society.[77] He used the image of a pyramid, with the more basic needs placed at the bottom. Once we acquire the basic levels of psychological and physical safety, we move up the pyramid, filling voids with the variances of love and esteem. Eventually, we arrive at the top, which he calls "self-actualization and transcendence."[78]

Maslow's Hierarchy of Needs

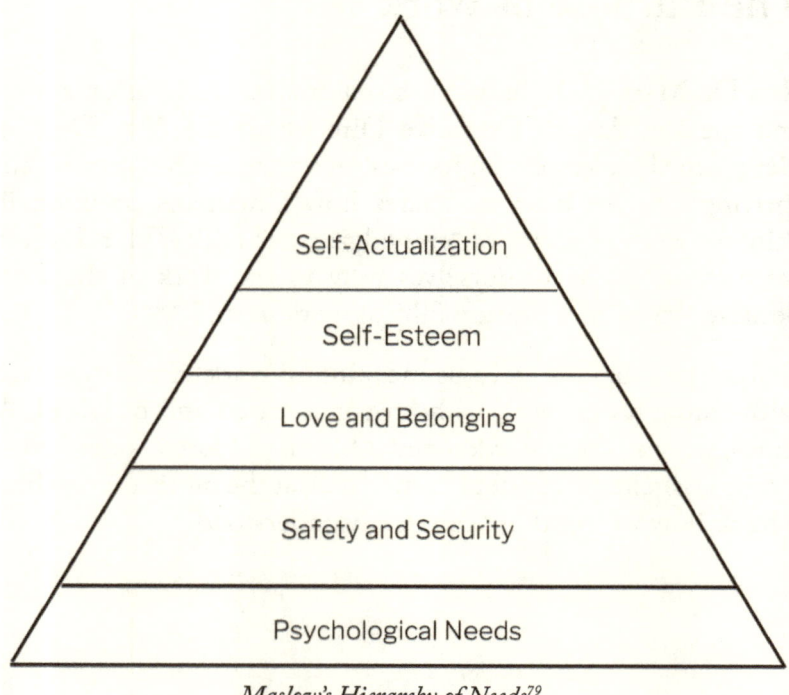

Maslow's Hierarchy of Needs[79]

Within Christian circles, we shy away from psychological trends or teachings. But the concept explains how and why the vocation of work causes friction in our pursuit of purpose. At the beginning of our human lives, we focus on those things that keep us safe. Working provides the necessary resources to survive. As we gain those and step up the needs pyramid, we focus more on other needs, like love and our identity.

Chapter 2 examined how we derive our identity from social and self-concepts. As we move up the ladder, we surpass necessity and move into passion. We must provide food, clothing, and shelter for ourselves and those we love. We're also called to serve a group of other humans who are created in God's divine image. But before we can do that, we must be able to provide for ourselves. Once we feel safe, we ask more complex questions like "What fuels me? What am I passionate about?"

And we launch our quest to find meaningful work.

Meaningful Work

In 2023, the Harvard Business Review examined the factors that make work meaningful. MIT Sloan interviewed 135 people who worked in 10 different occupations. They were asked to share stories or times when they found their work meaningful.

In general, meaningful work tends to be personal and individual.[80] "We have defined meaningful work as arising 'when an individual perceives an authentic connection between their work and a broader transcendent life purpose beyond the self.'"[81]

We derive meaningful work from several places. The meaning of work can come from an organizational purpose, a task, a job, or our interactions. The vision of our company or ministry can give our work meaning. We find purpose in our tasks or jobs like writing software or feeding the homeless. We also find fulfillment in working with like-minded people who share a common goal.

For example, purpose is not found in the military's tasks. Driving a truck or monitoring radio traffic doesn't provide a deep sense of purpose. Most days, the tasks are draining and mundane. But the people are the purpose. Serving alongside those who stand arm in arm with us is the point. Their safety keeps us going on hard days. And in each of those situations, there is an opportunity for us to rely on the promises of God.

As a certified career and business coach, I've spent hours speaking with people about their careers and goals. We strive to be good stewards of time and resources and seek a passion-filled life. Often, we arrive at an intersection with empty hands.

But why is their vocational journey so difficult? Because the pursuit of purpose causes anxiety and pressure when we focus on three things: the meaning of work, performance-based faith, and our fear of failure.

Vocation outside of full-time ministry is not against God's design. We can be God-honoring Christians and work in the secular world. The world needs successful businesses, life-giving schools, safe medical facilities, and an ethical government. These elements make up the world, our communities, and the church.

But don't take my word for it; let's dig into the Scriptures and explore the biblical basis of work.

The Biblical Basis of Work

We see the concept of work laid out in biblical principles across both the Old and New Testaments. In Genesis 2:15, God took man and placed him in the Garden of Eden to work and care for it. The word work is *avondah*,[82] used 289 times in the Old Testament. It is often translated into three words: worship, serve, or work.

When we consider worship, does vocation come to mind?

Close your eyes.

Envision a place or space where you've lost yourself in the abundant and amazing feeling of worship. You offer your complete self to a holy God.

Does your place of business or job enter that space? For many people, the answer is no!

As we revisit our idea of a paradox discussed in Chapter 1, we see the theme return.

Remember that:

- War is peace.
- Freedom is slavery.
- Ignorance is strength.

But now we can add another example: work is worship.

Our jobs are not designed to give us purpose. If God has already defined our purpose, how can we replace our perspectives and live in the promises of God each day as it relates to our vocation? The answer: by deciding to live a life where **work is worship!**

There's a great honor in committing to good works: Fighting terrorism, ending slavery, and helping to ease or end the suffering of others through teaching, education, medicine, or charity offers hope and love to the world. The actions aren't inherently evil or wrong. We must consider work within the context of the mission, the ministry, and the marketplace.

Mission

Paul was a Jew whom God called to minister to the Gentiles because of his background and role. But he was also a tentmaker. He learned how to work with his hands (1 Corinthians 4:12) and spent the remainder of his ministry traveling, growing the church, and working at a trade. In Galatians, Paul reminds us that a man reaps what he sows (Galatians 6:7). God instructs us to go to the world and let our works, hands, and actions be fruitful in His name.

But the trap is when we look at our performance and make that more about purpose than serving God.

Ministry

During Jesus's ministry, many people joined His team. There are several references in the New Testament where the women who traveled with Jesus started businesses to support His ministry. The Apostle Luke tells us:

After this, Jesus traveled about from one town and village to another, proclaiming the good news of the kingdom of God. The Twelve were with him and also some women who had been cured of evil spirits and diseases: Mary (called Magdalene) from whom seven demons had come out; Joanna, the wife of Chuza, the manager of Herod's household; Susanna; and many others. These women were helping to support them out of their own means" (Luke 8:1–3 NIV).

The women, among others, provided physical and financial resources to help Jesus's ministry. Their work became their worship.

Marketplace

Possibly one of the most encouraging references, or the one that causes women in the church to struggle with purpose anxiety, is the Proverbs 31 woman. In Proverbs 31, we see the woman rise early. She has a business, takes care of her home, and is a busy woman.[83]

She considers a field and buys it;
out of her earnings, she plants a vineyard.

She sets about her work vigorously;
her arms are strong for her tasks.

She sees that her trading is profitable,
and her lamp does not go out at night.

These three stories extract examples of ways or reasons to work as unto the Lord. Often, we look at the job or vocation we pursue and derive value from it. That value system is skewed based on our biases and social perspectives. Every job can be a parable to show the world God's righteousness. We just need to shift our focus to see their value.

Every Job a Parable

In his book *Every Job a Parable*, John Van Sloten explains how all work matters to God because all work can reflect some aspect of His character. He explains that engineers, florists, landlords, police officers, bakers, and sanitation workers are a "kind of parable, where God lives out and speaks through our lives."[84] He explains how Jesus used parables to tell us stories about God's revelation via creation. The creational goodness of a specific job can be found in the parables of Jesus. Jesus speaks to and through us through our unique expression of work. "God intended work by a means in which we can know Him."[85]

So, if work is an expression of God in us, why do we put so much pressure and attention on it?

Let's take our friend John, who is a doctor, again. He studied and spent countless hours with little sleep and copious amounts of coffee, performing late-night rounds as a hospital resident.

His passion for helping the world is righteous and honorable, but John is frustrated.

Does he focus on the promises of God, or is his focus on the performance and purpose that he finds in his career? If it's the latter, we see frustration emerge even though he's pursuing an honorable career.

As Christians, our job is not designed to *give* us purpose. Our purpose is found in God alone. Remember, we have two tasks: to love the Lord with our entire heart, soul, mind, and strength and to love our neighbor as ourselves. You can do that by being a doctor, of course. But can you do it by being a supply person working a late-night shift at Waffle House? Can you do it by driving an Uber? Absolutely.

It requires us to shift our perspective from performance to promise.

Shifting from Performance to Promise

The first step in shifting from performance to promise is acknowledging that purpose is not found solely in our job. Our duty title does not define us, which is hard to grasp. Some of us, like warriors, caregivers, teachers, or doctors, have dedicated much of our lives to a profession or career. We're committed to a craft.

But our vocations and ministries are the conduits through which we show God's love to the world. If we see our vocation as the branch to offer God's love to the world and not view it as our purpose, then we can find the peace of knowing we're walking in God's promises.

The second step is to release our identity. We cling to our vocation or role because we find our identity so tightly knit inside it. Do we believe God would give us something else or be glorified if we chose to do something else? We grapple with a scarcity mindset, which limits our ability to see past performance and focus on the promises of each day.

And when upsetting times come, like job loss, disability, or even career growth, we carry the anxiety and pressure that we somehow feel like we will make the wrong decision or upset the purpose apple cart.

Does God want you to be a doctor? I don't know, friend, but after living over 40 years on this earth and watching people I love navigate vocational or ministry events, amid many other things, I have realized that vocations, like many other things, are temporary.

Our perception of God changes when we find value in performance instead of His promises. Today, culture offers a toxic cycle of performance-based faith. It directly and indirectly affects our perception of God and our roles and purpose on this Earth, both inside and outside the church.

When we focus on performance instead of promises, we miss God moving in all things, calling us into a deeper communion and compassion with Him. The desire to develop a heart that mirrors the Father's is a righteous charge. We must first focus on removing the roadblocks that keep us locked in our purpose puzzle. We begin by replacing a legalistic, performance-based faith with a humble heart.

Let's define and understand how legalism affects our expectations of purpose.

The Toxic Cycle of Performance-based Faith

We are inundated with rules and regulations: Don't pass go, only pass on the left, etc. The list seems endless. But the laws of the road, for example, are in place so that we can safely travel from one location to another without causing harm to ourselves or others. In the Old Testament, God gave the Law to the Israelites to protect them. But He also wanted to commune with His people, which couldn't be accomplished after the fall of man.

In the Sermon on the Mount, Jesus explains that He came to fulfill the laws (Matthew 5:17). He taught us how to strive to live. However, over time, denominations or congregations identify their expectations for how Christians should behave.

Humans perpetuate legalism. Not always by intention, but Dr. Burk Parsons, the senior pastor of St. Andrew's Chapel in Sanford, Florida, explains that "legalism draws attention to us, but gospel religion draws attention to Jesus Christ."[86] In various forms of legalism, churches define the "values and practices, that are not biblically explicit, which, for better or worse, are expected of individuals in the local congregation."[87] Those differences are often not black or white, right or wrong topics. But they shape our perspectives on purpose and performance.

Over time, people tire of trying to live up to the standards set by the church or navigating the expectations that are either said or unsaid. Culture determines how we act; we've discussed it before. Like the identity iceberg, our belief system regarding how we should perform is also rooted in the culture of our churches and religious teachings—those appointed as the authority to govern and rule.

Congregants become tired of the pressure and unmet expectations. Anxiety ensues because, quite frankly, we're looking at everyone in our circle and comparing ourselves to them. We ask, "What's wrong with me?" but the answer is probably "nothing." It's your standard or expectation that needs to change.

After navigating that teeter-totter Christian life, people can find themselves between passivity and production on various sides of the spectrum. Both are equally damaging when we strive to live in the promises of God.

Passivity vs. Production

On the passivity side of the scale, Christians become exhausted from navigating accountability expectations. Over time, we may withdraw from engaging with our faith community. Conversely, *when focus and emphasis are on fulfilling the great dream rather than loving one another and the world, we have opened the door to a master-slave spirit.*[88]

When we measure success, we look for output or productivity. If we produce a lot of fruit, we believe it results from diligent work. But it doesn't. It comes from abiding in the vine—the life source. If we focus purely on our output, we become slaves to the process. We must, in turn, focus on faith and remain humble in word and deed. We must practice the art of biblical humility.

Biblical Humility

Do you consider yourself ambitious? In Christian circles, ambition can be considered a form of carnal pride.[89] Church culture says, as Dr. Stephen Crosby explains, Christians are expected to "be polite and don't put yourself forward."[90] We consider this lack of ambition to be an example of holding a godly character. Crosby contends that the "ultimate act of biblical humility is confident faith. It is the abandonment of confidence in oneself and utter confidence in God and His promises."[91] He believes our failure to act on God's promises is due to insecurity, fear, or psychological maladjustment, and it is not biblical humility.

How does all this fit together in our pursuit of purpose?

The culture of performance-based faith, coupled with our misguided or misunderstood belief in the vocation of work, shapes our behaviors. It is because of those elements that we experience purpose anxiety and fear. The performance that encourages us to climb the ladder can cause a great degree of anxiety and stress. In Part 2, I offer some self-examination questions to consider as you seek to determine if you're struggling with performance-based faith.

When we think about performance, the third element of the purpose paradigm is learning how achievements and accolades shape our perspective.

The Perfectionist Trap

I excelled in school. It was my safe place. For the perfectionist daughter of an alcoholic, I sought out ribbons and achievements. For many years, they became my identity. When I entered the military, the budding perfectionist thrived. The military offered organization and structure. When I succeeded, they provided medals to wear on my chest.

But over the years, as I became a mother and wife, the perfectionist caused great strife in my home. And in the end, the walls and straight lines came crumbling down around me.

What if we break down these purpose barriers and reframe our mindset and ability to find peace, purpose, and provision with God daily?

In that case, we must acknowledge when we find value in our achievements. At times, through them, we strive to collect crowns that last forever.

A Crown That Lasts Forever[92]

Does God care about crowns? The Scriptures tell us He does.

James 1:12 reminds us of the Lord's promise: *Blessed is the one who perseveres under trial because, having stood the test, that person will receive the crown of life that the Lord has promised to those who love him.*

But at times, storing up crowns in heaven is discomforting. It makes me feel selfish and full of pride.

At least until I understood the concept.

Author and pastor Chuck Swindoll helps us understand this concept in his New Testament Insights series, described in the book *Insights on Revelation.*[93]

The New Testament mentions five "heavenly crowns" for believers. These are future rewards offered for faithfulness in our earthly life. These are the Crowns of Exaltation (1 Thess. 2:19), Righteousness (2 Tim. 4:8), Life (James 1:12, Rev 2:10; 3:11), Imperishability (1 Cor. 9:25), and Glory (1 Pet. 5:4).

The table below is an excerpt from his book explaining the crown and reward.

Crown	Bible Reference	Reward
Crown of Exultation	1 Thess. 2:19	For those who win others to Christ
Crown of Righteousness	2 Tim. 4:8	For those who live in the expectation of Christ's coming
Crown of Life	James 1:12; Rev. 2:10; 3:11	For those who endure persecution until death
Crown of Imperishability	1 Cor. 9:25	For those who run in a race of life in purity and self-control
Crown of Glory	1 Pet. 5:4	For those who lead the church in humility

Christians often say, "You're storing up crowns in heaven." Is that true? I don't know for sure. But in this Scripture, I find clarity on what was intended by the references used.

If we consider our pursuit of purpose, it's clear when and how crowns are rewarded:

- Lead others to Christ
- Live in the expectation of Christ's return
- Endure persecution until death - the Martyr
- Run a race of purity and self-control
- Lead the church with humility

How do you navigate between crowns and living in the promise? There's a significant risk when we consider performance-based faith. When we focus on storing up crowns in heaven, our performance becomes more important than seeing and living in the promises of God each day.

Our last challenge when considering how purpose becomes performance is the fear of failure. We must overcome the fear of failure through God's unconditional love.

Breaking the Stronghold of Fear

Another manifestation of legalist disease is a stronghold of fear. Legalists live under the constant and nagging fear of God's rejection due to disappointing Him or missing His will. We fear the rejection that comes from making mistakes. We fear the punishment for failure or inadequacy associated with earthly relationships.[94]

Still, we know that accomplishments or failures do not last. We've read this a hundred times and heard it in a thousand sermons, but it still causes us anxiety.

It's okay to struggle with your identity. It's OK if performance has become your purpose or if it feels wrapped together in a messy ball of spaghetti.

It's okay.

Acknowledging the Struggle

This is the next step in a journey where we acknowledge our struggle with purpose and performance. We admit that our achievements cause us to put our focus on our job, ministry, and performance. When we do that, we take our eyes off of our Savior.

It's tough to lay down something you've built and labored to attain. Finding your identity in it takes work. Everyone has a degree of pride. The challenge is to balance on the teeter-totter between pride and confidence.

God calls us to be confident in Him. It becomes a daily journey to lay down our performance and identity before the Lord and ask if they are for Him. In this season of my life, I've decided that I no longer wish to carry them.

> **GOD CALLS US TO BE CONFIDENT IN HIM.**

At the Feet of Jesus

There was a season in our lives when we struggled. *Struggle* is a word that bookends most of my life. But in that season, I searched for the Lord.

One night, with my journal in my lap, I sat in the quiet space, seeking the Lord's voice.

I wrote "God" in the circle of the page. Around it, I drew lines like a spoke on a wheel. In each space, I listed the "good things" we were doing.

The kids attended Christian school, we served in the ministry, and we were active church members. I led Bible study and worked at a good job serving the military. My husband was on active duty.

These were all good things. So, why were we so frustrated if we were doing such good things? Why was there so much anxiety in our home?

When I laid all of those before the Lord, I prayed, not knowing that our lives would be radically changed in a few months. In my journal, I wrote, "Lord, are these for you or me? Because if they are for you, then please use them. And if they are for me, I need you to take them away."

Today, only two remain.

We left our church and our ministry service, the kids changed schools, we moved three counties away, and we left our jobs.

Everything changed.

All that remains is the pregnancy ministry and our family. Everything else ended.

And do you know what? We are fine. But we didn't see it like that at the time.

For months, my husband and I returned to our old community church. We drove an hour and a half on Sunday to worship with our friends, trying to stay connected with our community. I drove back and forth to Bible studies and worship team practice to stay connected. I thought these were what God had called us to, so it must not be time to lay them down.

But the burden became too great.

At one point, I realized they were not where God had called us anymore. God had called us to a new community, church, and town. And in that place, we were supposed to make new friends. We were supposed to live and build a life with new people, which was heartbreaking because I thought we were losing everything.

Everything was falling apart. Everything that I thought God was in seemed to be washing away. And with it, my identity, if I'm honest.

One Sunday, my husband looked at me and said, "This can't be all God has for us, Danita. If it is, then it isn't true to His character."

Oh, how right he was! It's been six years since Mark made that statement, and oh, how things have changed! Other than the pregnancy help ministry, everything else is gone. Our jobs, churches, schools, and friends all changed. Some elements or people remain, but many are gone. And do you know what? God's love and His promises remain steadfast and evermore.

Steadfast Love

For almost 30 years, I've served the Department of Defense in various roles and fashions. I joined the Air Force during my senior year of high school and spent most of my adult life serving the armed forces. Over the years, I realized how much my identity was tied to my military career.

The military shaped me. It gave me focus, values, and a future. But the danger in that offering was more significant than I understood.

"I'm a warrior" is a statement I've shared many times. The role of a warrior is one society respects. We honor it by offering a "thank you" when a soldier or first responder visits a restaurant wearing their uniform. Serving in the military is a calling like missionary, pastor, or teacher. We stand in the gap, offering to protect those who cannot protect themselves. We believe in justice and strive to protect the world.

But the deception on our purpose journey arises when we place our value on our performance.

You don't have to work or serve in the military for this to be a challenge. When we let our identity and performance drive our beliefs and concepts of purpose, at some point in our lives, we will each face the finality and frailty of it.

Our vocations or ways we serve become a deep part of who we are. If we try to lay down the pursuit of purpose and strive to live each day in the promises of God, then we must lay our identity and performance on the table.

The last chapter discussed how we rediscover our identity in Christ. But a significant part of our identity and purpose, or at least our perception of meaning, lies in what we do.

The church is not immune to it. We call it performance-based faith, legalism, or idolatry. But the foundation is the same. When we struggle with our pursuit of purpose, our performance is a significant roadblock to overcoming anxiety and finding peace in Him.

During COVID-19, like many others, I lost my job. I'd had foot surgery, and then a few days after, as I sat home on convalescent leave, I received a 15-minute notice that my job would be terminated effective immediately.

For the next three weeks, I sat immobilized in my chair in my bedroom and cried. I cried because I had lost my job, couldn't walk, and had no idea what to do. As you can imagine, it was a tough time for me. But I realized that more than the loss of income or title, I had lost a great sense of my identity and value. When we tie our identity and values to our jobs, we struggle when they are gone. But the commonality of it doesn't diminish the impact it has on our lives, faith, and our walk with God.

Walking with the Savior

Amid this striving, performance-based culture, God offers you beautiful grace. As His children, we grow, serve, love, build, and restore. We strive to be good stewards of the resources His love provides. There's nothing wrong with that. But we should allow grace, humility, and empathy to prevail.

Don't miss the divine, holy promises of Jesus Christ standing beside you daily.

As you strive to walk with the Savior daily, remember why and what you're building. Consider why you strive and surrender to the performance of your careers. When challenging times come, or you start to focus on your performance, remember the promises of the Lord.

Proverbs 16:3 reminds us to commit to the Lord whatever we do, and He will establish our plans. We "commit ourselves to the works of the Lord."

Work or vocation is one of the largest consumers of time and energy. But the Lord directs our steps. Our direction and contentment come in the daily surrender of trusting God with our work. Timothy reminds us, "The aim of our charge is love that comes from a pure heart, a good conscience, and a sincere faith" (1 Timothy 1:5).

A Prayer to Break the Stronghold of Performance

Dear Lord,

Please allow me to see myself through Your sovereign eyes. Give me the supernatural peace and confidence to work as unto You, as I carry only those items You have called me to bear. May Your wisdom and discernment guide my daily steps. May I find grace and clarity in You. May You bless the work of my hands, business, and ministry to bring hope and love to the world. May all glory be Yours, forever and ever.

Amen.

THE SANCTITY OF SUFFERING

And through the tears, God begins to smile.

—Dalai Lama, *The Book of Joy*

N orth Carolina, which I now call home, ushers in the spring with a pesky cloud of pollen. It hangs in the air, swarming around our cars like a caricature of bees bent on wreaking havoc on innocent bystanders. After a few moments, these yellow "cartoon clouds" dance across the sky, leaving chaos in their wake. Eyes swell, noses run, and cars disappear under the grimy blanket. For humans, they are most inconvenient. But for the plants and forest surrounding my home, pollen brings new life.

Life's hardest moments are like pollen clouds. We are inclined to nix their value. At times, they leave us with sticky hands and swollen eyes, but they also bring new life. We miss how they contain God's promises. Like the pollen clouds moving across my backyard, tough times unveil the promise that God comforts those in need.

We often seek the purpose in our pain. It seems complex at times. Wrought with years of fear or hurt, the weight of it is too great to bear. But carrying the weight is not the point. We can miss the promise if we get lost in seeking the purpose of painful moments. That quest only causes the storm to build inside us.

God's promises are more profound and intimate than our words can define. Promises are covenants that God made with His people. They are the root and foundation that we hold. We cling to them when the waves of life smack us against the shoreline. Our bodies drag across rocks of broken fragments, gathering scrapes and bruises. We cling to them like a life raft on rough waters because we are weary even when the Creator calls us beloved. And deep inside, we ask, "Do You see me, Lord? Am I worthy of Your love? What am I good for?" His response is anything but "absolutely nothing."

Comfort is God's promise that we are never alone.

The Promise of Comfort

In our pursuit of purpose, we must surrender the questions that plague our minds and hearts. We find a simple, eternal truth that allows us to find the peace of knowing we are forever held in the sovereign Savior's arms.

We no longer need to ask, "What is my purpose?" because we have His promises. And the promises sustain us. We replace our pursuit of purpose with the promises of God's truth.

- We cling to the promise of God's eternal love.
- We survive in the promise of Jesus's resurrection.
- We surrender to the promise of God's never-ending, too-big-to-hold forgiveness.
- We bond to the promise that God bore us in His image.
- We fasten to the promise that God will never leave us nor forsake us.

- We bind to the promise that despite what we see, God is always bigger.

We will explore these more in Part 3 as we learn how to walk in the promises of God. But for now, remember this: God is bigger than cancer or death. That doesn't mean we will never suffer. When such things come to us, what do we do?

After navigating the global pandemic, many people came face to face with the finality of life. This life. The only one that we get to live on this side of heaven. We faced our busy lives, self-defeating jobs, messy homes, and short-sighted faith. In those moments of—as they call it—"the great reset," many people (including me and those I love) stopped and asked, "Why?"

While many were asking, "Why is this happening?" others asked, "Why am I living my life this way?" or better yet, "What do I need to change to live a life by divine design?"

A Life by Divine Design

One night I fell asleep, praying for a miracle.

Do you ever do that? Do you pray for healing, restoration, or an end to the suffering you see?

I did. I woke up the following day hoping her cancer was gone. But it wasn't.

Sometimes, you have to fall asleep in the arms of Jesus. His love is the only balm our wounds can withstand; it never stings and only soothes. It heals. It restores. Even amid great pain, His love makes all things new.

Ecclesiastes reminds us that "everything is beautiful in its time."[95] But unlike our perceptions, new doesn't always mean shiny. God's love restores that which is tarnished or rusted.

We love the hope of restoration. That's why we love renovation projects: old cars, houses, or our affinity for *Antique Road Show* or *American Pickers*. We love the possibility that something old can be found, restored, and deemed worthy of having value.

Do you see that connection with our lives and our pain? We apply hope to our heartache and our definition of purpose. In life's most challenging moments, we crave to believe that our pain has value. We say that "everything happens for a reason." It's as if we believe our pain is orchestrated by a diabolical puppet master in the cosmos, pulling strings and moving people for his pleasure.

The Purpose of Pain

The question of purpose, as it relates to pain, is a common question. We ask, "Why did this happen?" and the world, or the church, often offers that "everything happens for a reason."

But in our pursuit of purpose, we must recognize how our suffering draws us and others closer to Him.

How can we survive the pain, receive His comfort, and pick ourselves up from the bathroom floor on tough or trying days? How does a person with a terminal diagnosis find hope in her pain? How does another release the daily weight and regret after having multiple abortions?

Do we offer empty apologies about the world's brokenness? No! God calls us to stand on His word and His character. He told us to (1) love Him with our entire heart, soul, mind, and strength and (2) love our neighbors as ourselves. What does that look like in times of great pain?

Friend, there are one billion ways to help ease the suffering of others. But first, we must realize that suffering and comfort go hand-in-hand in the kingdom.

In 2 Corinthians 1:3–5, Paul encourages the church in Corinth in its struggles. He says, "We give the comfort we receive to help others. For as we share abundantly in Christ's sufferings, so through Christ, we share abundantly in comfort too."

When we feel lost or alone, we're isolated, confused, and unable to understand our pain. But in the kingdom algorithm, suffering is not isolated. It does not exist alone, nor is it separated from the comfort of God.

> *Because he has suffered when tempted,*
> *he can help those being tempted.*
>
> Hebrews 2:18

In this promise, great hope exists for those who suffer. Knowing that God did not leave us in our pain is the greatest joy. James encourages us to count it all joy when we meet various kinds of trials.[96] But his offering needs to make more sense in the context of our lives. The formula doesn't add up in our human brains.

That's why we must replace our understanding with His promises.

The Comfort Algorithm

I think about so many friends and loved ones who have or continue to suffer. They struggle with past abuse, cancer, and toxic work conditions. They navigate the pain of infertility, miscarriage, and abortion. They grieve lost loved ones. They've lost jobs, navigated pandemics, and tried to revive crumbling businesses. All the while, they attempted to reconcile their pain with some sense of purpose. They seek an answer to the "What is my purpose?" question, hoping that a simple formula will be revealed to explain the reason for their suffering. They desire a simple answer from God: Here's why I did this (a), and this is how it will be made right (b).

But that's not how the kingdom works.

Returning to the Scriptures, we see how God simply says, "I will meet you in your suffering. I will bring you comfort so that you may comfort others."

The purpose of pain is to help ease the suffering of others. That may be the only part of the equation that is always true. In this regard, A + B always equals C.

A (suffering) + B (love of Christ) = C (Comfort to the world).

> ## A (SUFFERING) + B (LOVE OF CHRIST) = C (COMFORT TO THE WORLD)

When we combine suffering with Christ's love, we always find comfort. It may not look like what we think it should, but it's always there.

When complicated times come, we ask clarifying questions: why, how, and what if. That's the normal grieving process. It's how our minds try to make sense of a difficult or terrifying situation.

But then God comes and brings His comfort to our lives, and we see that the question we're asking is wrong. It isn't so much a question of why this happened. But more, where are You, Lord? I can't see You.

It's like the song in the 2000 movie, *How the Grinch Stole Christmas,* which searches for Christmas as if it can't be found. When we enter this place, we can't see God. Our minds try to reconcile this pain with a purpose, but we are left empty and seemingly alone. But the Scriptures tell us we are not alone. I am not alone in my suffering. He is the God who sees me.

The Story of Moses

If there were anyone in Scripture who could tell a nail-biting story, it would be Moses.

Moses was the son of an Israelite. He was placed in the river, a baby in a basket, because his mother feared for his life.

Pharaoh decreed that all the Israelite children should be murdered upon their birth. But the midwives refused. And so, instead of ending the child's life, they placed him in a basket and pushed him down the river.

Pharaoh's daughter picked him up and raised him in the palace as royalty. But soon after he became an adult, he found great pain in the way the Egyptians treated the Israelites. And so, in his rage, he killed an Egyptian and buried the body.

Once he was discovered, Moses fled to the wilderness. In that place of fear and isolation, God revealed Himself to him. An angel of the Lord appeared in a flame of fire out of the midst of the bush. God said, "Come, I will send you to Pharaoh so you can bring my people out of Egypt."[97]

Moses felt unequipped, but he agreed to try. It wasn't an easy journey. For years, Moses suffered many things, but God was with him in each moment. The greater our pain, the closer the Savior is to our hearts.

The more I see the world's hurt and pain, the more I realize that the question, "What is the purpose of this pain?" is the wrong one to ask.

We can only hope to draw nearer to the Father's heart. In that drawing, we find peace. God is faithful to His promises, and what He promises to His people—salvation, life, and inheritance—is eternal and incorruptible.[98]

Jesus tells us that He is with us always. Our identity is in Him—always—from the very core and fiber of our beings.

I knit you together.[99]

I know your name.[100]

Countless Scriptures describe God's divine power, wonder, and strength and teach us about His sovereignty and love.

So, if this is the God who sees us, truly sees us in all our vulnerable, human futility, then why can't we find simple answers to our purpose questions? The Gospel of Matthew says, "Ask and you shall receive, seek and you shall find, knock and the door shall be opened unto you."[101] This is the entire basis of faith. This statement tells us how we find the answers – even the messy ones.

God's big enough for you to ask Him the upsetting questions. He's not going anywhere. When did we get to the place where we thought that the sovereignty of God precluded us from crawling right into the lap of our Savior and asking Him tough questions like "Where did constellations come from? Or why did my mommy die?"

Those are questions the Creator can handle. Trust me. He created the heavens and the earth with His breath. He can handle our questions. In the seeking, we find information to change our perspectives about who He is and what He has called us to do.

Shifting Perspectives

We must change our perspectives about what we consider valuable in the kingdom equation.

Value comes in many forms. We often consider the newest product to have the greatest value. But restoration is important. Reframing our perspective to see a different view of what we thought was lost and old can be restored. It can be used to provide something of value to others. We need to reframe our perspective.

God is a God of restoration. In the Scriptures, He restores His children to their rightful place. He changes their name, giving them a new home and identity. But He doesn't take away their past. He doesn't erase it. He uses it as the catalyst for change. He uses it in the wilderness so they can grow. He uses it to draw them to serve a community of suffering people.

- Moses suffered for the Israelites.
- Paul suffered with grief from having killed Christians.
- John suffered for Jesus' sake—persecution, isolation.
- Sarah suffered from infertility, infidelity, and jealousy.
- Naomi suffered from the loss of her husband, home, and family.
- Esther suffered from the schemes to kill the Jews.
- Jesus was the greatest sufferer of all.

In each of these situations, God used their suffering to comfort others.

Instead of asking God to take away the pain or to identify the purpose of this horrible thing, ask God to show you how your suffering can bring comfort to others. Or better yet, ask to draw nearer to the Father's heart. We lay in the arms of Jesus. That's all. We allow the Savior to soothe our wounds. One day, the time may come when we find a way to let our suffering comfort others. But it's not required. We must trust in His promises above all else.

Forged in Fire

For centuries, blacksmiths met the demands of their communities by applying heat and pressure to different metals to create necessary tools and hardware. The wagon wheel is a prime example. Before the invention of metal wheels, wagons traveled on wooden frames. As they were phased out, forged iron wheels became more reliable and desired.

We're not as concerned about the history of wheelmaking as we are about using heat and pressure to create necessary tools. Without the fire and pressure of the roaring coals and the hammer, metal cannot bend. But that process must have a focus. It must have a goal. Metal can be formed into a valuable tool with time and pressure. The same is true for our perception of purpose.

In 2016, author and professor Angela Duckworth[102] taught us about the concept of *grit*. Her research spanned teaching, business consulting, and the study of neuroscience. She concluded that our success is driven by passion and long-term perseverance, not just intelligence or knowledge.

Expanding upon her research, we find the *grit* to overcome today's hardship because we see **hope** for the future. We see light at the end of the tunnel. We believe our moments of pain or hurt matter, and someone values our contribution to the world.

When we are seen in all our human forms, our hurts, pain, hopes, and dreams matter to the world. In that space, there is hope. There is a purpose. But in that process, we can lose sight of the most important thing: A holy God, walking in the world, fully man, fully divine, dying for us.

That is the most important thing.

As Christians, we give all of ourselves to Him. Every step, moment, heartache, and fear is for His glory, His purpose, and His way of showing His love to the world. When our days on this earth end, that is the point.

When my father died, I found great comfort in the Bible. Page after page showed me the sovereignty of God and that during my greatest pain, He was with me. I would see God in all things for a year after Daddy died. It was like my emotional senses were on overdrive. I could feel Him in the wind, the trees, the sunlight, and the rain. I sat in His presence and knew God saw me in my suffering.

> AS CHRISTIANS, WE GIVE ALL OF OURSELVES TO HIM. EVERY STEP, MOMENT, HEARTACHE, AND FEAR IS FOR HIS GLORY, HIS PURPOSE, AND HIS WAY OF SHOWING HIS LOVE TO THE WORLD. WHEN OUR DAYS ON THIS EARTH END, THAT IS THE POINT.

That is the greatest comfort of all. Today, four years later, as time edges closer to the anniversary date of his passing, I remember how far I've come. I remember the moment in the early morning darkness when the telephone rang, and I heard my stepmother say, "Danita, your dad is gone. His heart gave out."

I remember the weight of grief in the first few days as I could barely function. I remember the stone feeling as I sat in the car with my daughter, unable to walk into the grocery store. Grief consumed me. I felt as if my legs were missing. The thought of getting out of the car seemed impossible because I couldn't carry the weight of my loss.

I remember weeks later, when we returned to our home church after the funeral, I stood on the steps with the pastor and shared my pain. I looked at the tears in my husband's crisp blue eyes as he wrestled with the pain of being unable to help me in my suffering.

And I remember the day his ashes came home to me as I sat on the porch on a warm Friday evening. I pulled the small blue urn from the package wrapped and prepared by my brother. I sat with him, the last physical part of my father, and we shared a beer on the porch, looking out across the still water and darkness of the forest behind my home. I sat with him—as close as our once human bodies could be—and I missed him beyond words or repair.

Today, I still see him—in the laughter of my children and my love of loud rock music, fast cars, and the open road on a sunny day. While it's not enough, I understand it. I released the control into the cosmos, saying to God on disagreeable days, "I love you still."

There is a sort of sanctity in our suffering that is hard to describe. I grieved all the "never had" moments for years after his death. I never had him walk me down the aisle on my wedding day. I never had him visit my home in North Carolina. I never had the chance to sit on the porch, fish in our pond, or walk around the forest with him. I never saw his face, sitting in the audience as my daughter and I led worship in our church. I never had the chance to show him the many years of work we've done in the pregnancy help ministry.

There are so many "never had" moments.

In my sadness, I could have asked God, "What is the purpose of his death?" But I've come to understand that a sovereign promise replaces my questions of purpose: "I will never leave you. I will bring comfort to those who suffer." Blessed are those who mourn, for they shall be comforted (Matthew 5:4).

God promises comfort. And in that promise, there is purpose. Because in that pain, I drew closer to Him. My heart, mind, soul, and strength yearn for His love to soothe my wounded heart. He is enough. The only comfort that truly heals.

If I spend my days, which is human and natural, asking about the purpose of this pain, I miss the very heart of the Father being offered to me.

The Heart of the Father

For years, I've served in the pregnancy help ministry. I've heard thousands of stories. Women who came into our center seeking refuge from a personal storm. Some come with unplanned pregnancies. Others suffer rape, molestation, or atrocious abuse. Others are women who lost their pregnancies through miscarriage or stillborn birth. And still others come who carry the secret and shame of abortion.

Their stories are as unique as the stars in the sky, but their pain is the same. And over the years, I've learned that God did not call me to end their suffering or save their lives. He called me to offer comfort to those in need.

Comfort looks different in each case, but it provides the greatest hope.

In a heart-wrenching season, my team offered comfort about a loss we were navigating. They said, "One day, we pray that God will use it for His glory." At that moment, I didn't care much for God's glory. I was raw and hurt. But as I sat and reflected on those words, I realized I needed to see the Father's heart.

> **NOT THE PURPOSE BUT THE PROMISE. I NEEDED THE PROMISE THAT HIS LOVE WAS ENOUGH.**

Not the purpose but the promise. I needed the promise that His love was enough.

In that moment of surrender, saw a small glimpse of His purpose. Pain allows us to see the Father's heart a little more with each passing day. And in the pain, there is always a promise that He is good.

Good, Good Father

If you've spent time in Christian circles, you've inevitably heard the music of Chris Tomlin. As a singer and songwriter, he blesses church venues with his powerful lyrics and complicated combinations of chord structures. You'll be hard-pressed to find a piano player who doesn't automatically say, "Oh, right, it's going to be hard because it's Chris Tomlin!" But you don't need to be a worship leader to recognize his name.

In 2016, Chris released his rendition of the song "Good, Good Father." Do you know the lyrics? The song is powerful.

One day, I sat at my computer digging through family videos. I clicked the icon and watched familiar faces flicker on my screen. It was a group of hopeful high school students crowded in our small Christian school gymnasium, preparing to depart on their first international mission trip. The class gathered in a semi-circle, preparing to sing as the family and staff prayerfully sent them to serve in Swaziland, Africa.

The hopeful students include my oldest daughter. She and her classmates worked each year to raise money to offset the cost of their senior mission trip. They delivered countless spaghetti dinners and painted Christmas canvases to travel abroad.

A few days before their departure, the school held a send-off assembly, where students and parents gathered in the small gymnasium to pray for their trip. Many left wide-eyed and full of wonder as they launched into the world! They spent a few weeks painting orphanages, traveling through the African wilderness, and learning how to be the hands and feet of Jesus.

It's been seven years since they boarded that plane and flew across the ocean to unknown worlds. But as I watched the video and heard their familiar voices singing, "You're a good, good Father," tears flowed down my cheeks.

I saw their hopeful, naive faces, but I now know the rest of the story.

In the years since their return, some suffered unspeakable hurt. Abuse, suicide, unplanned pregnancies, and car accidents are a few of the stories that come to mind as the video pans across the small gymnasium, and I make out their familiar faces, all wearing bright orange sweatshirts, singing to the beat of a trash can drum.

For some, their faith waxed and waned like a crescent moon. They questioned the love, grace, or sovereignty of a God who promised to love and protect them. It's easy to see why some ran so far from the church today. I understand why their disappointment, criticism, and disdain for religion run deep within their bones.

Others cling to grace like a life raft, begging it to protect them when the seas and storms of this world threaten to throw them out into the depths from which they cannot return.

I understand both perspectives: from those who cling and those who can't.

Purpose, or this quest for it, is pointless without God's promises. No matter what we strive to do or how diligently we work at protecting ourselves and our loved ones from the pain of this world, it's impossible to escape it unscathed.

In those moments, we ask what we should have done differently and where God's purpose is now.

But in the silence, we are only left with promises. We're only left with the promise that God said, "I will never leave you." In Jesus' suffering, we see how to share our pain with Him. This transfusion is enabled, face to face, bruise to bruise, blood to blood, and tear to tear, as our life mixes with His, and we become one.

The more I walk with Jesus, the harder it gets sometimes to hear His voice. But I know that He's always there. And when the world doesn't make sense, I trust in His promises because those are the only things I can cling to.

His promises teach me that God's purpose is not to make us suffer but to comfort us in that suffering. If we're honest or able to lift our heads above the cloudy confusion, there is a sort of beauty to it. In it, we are blessed to glimpse His hand as it holds our hearts.

The promise, the one that says that I will always love you, never ends.

The Prayer for The Brokenhearted

Dear Lord,

Raise Your mantle so all who suffer can draw closer to You. Let me only carry on that which You have divinely chosen. Let me see You in all my hurt and sadness. May You help me to see that the pain is not the purpose. Your love will always be enough. Please give me hope for tomorrow and the strength to draw closer to You.

Amen.

THE FREEDOM TO SURRENDER

The ultimate key to freedom is to keep becoming who you indeed are.

—Edith Eger, *The Gift*

I n the spring of 1944, Dr. Edith Eger lived in Kassa, Hungary, with her parents and two older sisters. At the time, she was a 16-year-old Hungarian Jew with no notion of the pain she would endure. War raged as semantic hatred spewed across the European landscape. Destruction scattered from Russia to Italy. In her book *The Gift*, she recounts her experiences.

Millions of Jewish prisoners were evacuated from their homes and marched from Poland through Germany to Austria. They performed slave labor in factories, riding on trains, and their bodies were used as human shields to protect cargo from British bombs.[103]

Seventy-five years after liberation from the Auschwitz camp, she still had nightmares and flashbacks. Despite the great pain of losing her parents to the gas chamber in Auschwitz, coupled with enduring unspeakable trauma as a prisoner, she found a way to find freedom in her extreme despair. She offers this foundational principle as her solution: **"The foundation of freedom is the power to choose."**[104]

Dr. Eger practiced finding freedom in her daily life. She explains that freedom requires two things. First, you must *acknowledge the awareness that suffering is temporary*, and second, you must clutch the *curiosity to discover what happens next.*[105]

148

She simply explains, "Hope allows us to live in the present instead of the past."[106]

Hope.

Freedom requires hope.

- Hope for tomorrow
- Hope for the future
- Hope to find beauty amid ashes

To shift our focus from the pursuit of purpose to God's promises, we must allow ourselves the freedom to surrender all that we are and have into His sovereign hands.

Jesus is our only hope. But surrendering and pursuing the intentional effort to find our hope in Jesus isn't always easy.

The Faith to Surrender

In the Scriptures, we watch the woman who bled for 12 years cling to the cloak of Jesus. Matthew 9:20–22 tells us that she told herself, "I will be healed if I can only touch his cloak."

Friend, that's faith.

Faith is the act of believing and not seeing. It's what drives us when everything around us tells us to turn the other way. When feelings and fears well up inside us, we hear the voice inside our head say, "What are you doing? Are you crazy? No, you can't possibly do this. You'll look foolish! Just sit back down." But in 1 Corinthians 1: 25, Paul says, "For the foolishness of God is wiser than human wisdom, and the weakness of God is stronger than human strength."

Paul reminds us that on God's worst day, He's wiser than all of our human wisdom and strength combined.

We can't rely solely on our feelings, thoughts, or emotions. Because on our best day, we pale in comparison to the Creator. We must have faith to believe in the things we cannot see.

As we follow the bleeding woman, we learn she knew this fear too well. But despite her fear, she found the faith to surrender all she had and believed in the power of Jesus.

Let's call her Laura. It's easier to relate to someone when we know their name.

The Story of Surrender

Imagine Laura sitting in a coffee shop in your community today. Imagine her alone, trying to reconcile the pain she carries in secret. That isolation makes her feel she doesn't deserve or have access to God's promises.

But that is simply untrue.

Laura finishes her soy latte and picks up her tattered shoulder bag filled with her newest Bible study, crumpled receipts from TJ Maxx, and a half-opened granola bar crushed at the bottom. She opens her car door and heaves it across to the passenger side of her blue Toyota Camry. She slides into the driver's seat, and then before she drops the car into drive, she lays her head on the steering wheel and sighs.

She's heard about these promises of God. She's heard the stories of this man named Jesus, who some believe is the Messiah. She *wants* to trust him. But she's been hurt. She's been isolated, and the world has told her she is unworthy.

She is unworthy of sitting at the table with others.

She is unworthy of sharing her pain with the crowds.

She is unable to speak about her past hurts and disappointments.

She carries the shame in secret, and the weight of it hangs around her neck like a millstone. She desires to be set free from it, but when she looks at her life and her purpose, all she can see is this pain.

Because she focuses on the pain, God's promises remain hidden from her sight.

But then something happens.

She decides to leave her only point of refuge. She tries with all her might to hold her world together, but at the core and fiber of her being, she knows she needs help.

So, she drives her car across town to glimpse Jesus. She hopes this man walking along the dusty street can relieve her pain.

The Act of Surrender

In her many years of suffering, she asked God, "Why? Why Lord? What is the purpose of this illness? Why will you not heal me? Why have you left me isolated, alone, and abandoned? Why have you left me discarded? Don't you see me, Lord?"

I imagine she fell asleep several nights in the arms of her God, *El Roi*, the one who sees. As she looked up into the night sky, surrounded by stars, did she ask him for a miracle? I think she did.

But the healing never came.

And then, we see her entering the town, getting out of her car, and pushing her way through the crowd so that she might get just the smallest glimpse of Jesus. Despite the cost of looking foolish, she chose to reach for him. She touches his cloak with a shaking hand, laying down everything she had because she had nothing left.

Surrender.

Do you see it? She laid down everything that she had *because* she had nothing left.

She came to the point in her journey where she realized that everything about her past, present, or future meant nothing without Jesus. Every moment of weakness. Every tear. Every glance. Every prayer. They meant nothing without him. Her *only and every* hope was in Him. And that promise, the promise of His love, ignited her heart. It gave her hope, strength, and purpose.

Let's sit in that space for a moment.

She had nothing left. Can you relate? I bet you can. I imagine there have been moments in the last week, month, or year when you've said, "I'm done." You told yourself or anyone listening that you couldn't continue.

For Laura, something about this moment is different. Something inside her decides to reach for Him despite her fear or shame.

A tiny flicker of hope starts to glow. She starts to see the warmth of His promise. That spark starts to smolder, and she believes she can replace the lie that she was not worthy with the promise that God's love is for her. Not just for them.

At that moment, she decides that only a touch of His cloak will heal her and make her whole again.

Laura abandons everything momentarily with the Savior—one small brush of His garment. She leaves her judgment and her shame on the sidewalk. She leaves her abuse and her isolation on the dusty side of the street.

She reaches for Him. *And she is healed.*

The Power of Surrender

If we consider the power of God's love and how Laura, the woman who bled for 12 years, can be healed with the simple touch of His garment, then how much more power does God's love provide?

We can only see a fraction of God's love for us. In our lives, and through our human lens, we only see a minuscule piece of the abounding joy and overwhelming pride God holds when He looks at us.

God is calling you, friend, just like He's calling me to stand, serve, give, love, and lean into contentious spaces. The Holy Spirit is at work – in your travels and in your circumstances. God doesn't ask for perfection because He doesn't need it. The blood of Jesus covered it all.

Jesus is only asking for your willingness to reach out and touch the edge of His cloak so that you, too, can be healed. But those acts of obedience come after the act of surrender. Before we can understand our purpose questions, we must surrender to this one simple fact: Jesus died for you. Surrender looks like acknowledging and believing that Jesus is enough in our hearts.

In that space, we find true peace. When we lay down our striving and expectations and see that His blood and grace cover us, we can see how God's sovereignty covers all things.

In that realization, there is the freedom to lay down all we carry and seek His promises above all else.

As Dr. Eger shared, finding freedom is a daily practice. We seek His promises daily, and in that endeavor, we find the peace and freedom our hearts truly desire.

A Life Surrendered

God is the sovereign hand that guides you always, even on your darkest days. And once we realize that simple yet eternal promise, we can unwrap the layers of our hearts to see the promises He offers each of us, like hidden treasures waiting to be found.

Inside the deepest layers of your heart is God's promise for you. Not me, not your neighbor or your spouse, or your children, your parents, or your friends. But solely for you.

Here are five ways to cultivate a daily practice to find the freedom to surrender to God's sovereignty.

1. Choose Your Hard

My sister-in-law is amazing. Over the years, I've watched her struggle to find her footing. One day, when we discussed the hardness of life, she offered this encouragement: "You have to choose your hard." She continued, "Life is hard. Everyone has something hard they have or want to do. But we get to choose. You must choose your hard because everything is hard."

- Being married is hard.
- Going to college is hard.
- Dropping out of school is hard.
- Having a baby is hard.
- Being alone is hard.

Choose your hard.

CHOOSE YOUR HARD.

I return to this statement when I'm having a particularly hard day. I've written it on a Post-it that sits on my bulletin board in my home office. "Choose Your Hard." It's a simple reminder that I can choose how to live each day.

So, friend, you get to choose your hard.

My hard looks different from yours, but our act of surrender is the same.

And in that action comes freedom. We receive the freedom to know that both the world's weight and the expectations of the outcome are not on our shoulders. We don't carry it. God carries it. We are merely vessels from which His love and grace are poured into the world.

If you shift your focus to searching out God's promises each day, you **will** find peace. You **will** live a purposeful life, but only because you know that you're resting in the arms of your Savior, a sovereign God who loves you and promises that love to you.

Jeremiah 29:11 says, "For I know the plans I have for you, declares the Lord, plans for peace and not for evil, to give you a future and a hope."

The Lord knew that we would struggle. He still knows how our minds and hearts seek clarity. And He reminds us that He will give us a future and hope.

2. Learn to Walk with the Savior

To replace the pursuit of purpose with the promises of God, we must act. Like our friend Laura, the woman who bled for 12 years, we too must reach for Jesus. There was a moment in her life when she decided that today would be different. She left the shadows and started walking toward the Savior.

God calls you and me to do that, friend; we are to walk with the Savior.

Learning how to walk with the Savior takes practice, commitment, and courage. The Savior's road is one no other human has walked before. The Savior carried the cross. I didn't. I'm just a girl who likes loud music, sunshine, and too much coffee. And sometimes, I say the F word when I'm having a particularly rough day.

When my children were small, we spent countless hours teaching them how to walk. Walking was one of their greatest feats! We tracked these milestones on calendars and at doctor's visits to show their progress. The more they could walk or talk, the closer they were to self-sufficiency.

But when they were little, they often fell. I remember countless trips to the kitchen or the emergency room, where we would whisk a sobbing toddler away for an exam. Sometimes, we needed stitches to repair a gaping head wound resulting from a fall in the garage or down an unsuspecting set of stairs.

As parents, we learn not to make any sudden movements. When they fall, we look unaffected. We blanket our response so that we don't scare them or make them more upset. It's a necessary part of growing up. In time and with practice, they learn to walk on their own.

Walking with the Savior is similar. At first, we might stumble down the road, kicking rocks or scraping our knees as we try to navigate this new road or life called "Being a Christian." But the walk gets easier as we learn how to balance our footsteps on holy ground.

Have you walked with the Savior on hard days, or are you just beginning to learn how to hear His voice? Has your journey with Jesus lasted five minutes, five months, or five years? Is your relationship new and budding, or would you consider yourself a solid friend of the Savior?

No matter how long you've walked with Christ, at some point, we all ask, "What is my purpose?" We consider this question part of our efforts to steward the time, talents, and treasures God has entrusted to our safekeeping. But that question must be rooted in the one foundational promise that surpasses them all: "Faith, hope, and love, but the greatest of these is love."[107]

Why do the Scriptures tell us that love is the greatest of all? If we dig deeper into the lessons from John, we see that we can only love "because He first loved us." That love, the sacrifice of God's coming to earth as a man to walk along dusty roads, to live our lives, eat our food, and hold our hands on heartbreaking, long, hot days, is the only way we can begin to understand how much God loves us.

Jesus surrendered all that He had for us. So, when life gets messy and we start to ask questions like "What is my purpose, Lord?" or "What is the purpose in this pain?" we start to take our eyes off Jesus and focus on ourselves. We must strive each day to focus on His promises more than anything else.

3. Take Time to Rest

Our life's purpose is not about pain. It's about God's promises of love, grace, provision, comfort, and redemption. By living in the peace of God's promises, you must strive to love yourself well.

When we stop striving for purpose, we realize we need rest. Sometimes, your heart needs rest. It needs to grieve, heal, and find the joy often lost in the hidden places where it hides.

Throughout our day, we show up, make the folders, sweep the floors, and feel accomplished. We take classes, write books, and manage projects, but we don't often see the wall of pain we carry. Our hearts are hurting. To replace the lie that purpose defines you, you must see and allow yourself to grieve and heal.

Healing takes time. The heart, like any other muscle or bone, must heal. But we can't see it.

So, take time to rest. Find a space to lay down the expectations and weight of the pain of our past and let God's light shine upon it.

4. Receive the Fruit of Healing

Healing comes in different forms and fashions. I wish it were immediate and a one-time event. But unfortunately, it's not. The older I get and the longer I walk with the Lord, the more I see how healing and spiritual maturity are elements that continue. They are cyclical. Never-ending. As Dr. Egers reminds us, "Healing is not linear."[108]

The world hurts you today; you grieve, get angry, accept, and allow that wound to heal. It's a never-ending process.

The journey from "I Love Jesus" to "Jesus Loves Me, This I Know" takes a lifetime. There is no perfect "get there" destination.

In his book *Redeeming Your Time,* Jordan Raynor discusses how God doesn't expect us to get everything done. That's not the point—your to-do list is not the point. And I think we sometimes forget that when we get busy doing "the things."[109]

I was confused, afraid, and relieved when reading this statement.

God doesn't expect me to "do" anything. Let that sink in. This is the most freeing revelation. God knows all the days of my life. They are numbered, just like he knows the number of hairs on my head.[110] What does God expect me to do if He knows all these things?

As Paul tells us, we know our life is not about work. It's about the saving grace of Jesus.[111] We also know that fruit represents our faith. So, as we grow in our spiritual maturity, we expect to see the fruit of that discipleship. But fruit can be something other than a product we produce. Fruit can be the way we handle conflict, the way we pray, and the way we carry joy.

Fruit *can* be in the form of healing. Here, we begin to see our purpose through our pain.

Sometimes, we believe our purpose is supposed to be what we *do.* We *do* serve and work. But if we focus solely on the *product rather than the practice,* we miss the entire point of everything.

Remember: God doesn't want or need you to *do* anything. He wants your heart first and *always.* And that action to give your heart to Jesus starts with the act of surrender.

But choosing to surrender is courageous. We must lay down the myths of insecurity and doubt. We must trust in God's character. Only then can we truly understand how God's promises change our perspective about purpose.

You get to choose to surrender. Change comes after acknowledging a problem. Like Laura, healing starts when you take the first step. And finding that first step often means listening to your heart.

5. Phone a Friend

In the late 1990s, *"Who Wants to Be a Millionaire"* aired on television. We watched Regis Philbin, the host, ask people to answer a series of questions to win a million dollars. In the segment, contestants could leverage a set of wild cards if they didn't know the answer. One of the best options was "phoning a friend." This sometimes proved problematic if the friend they chose wasn't an expert, but it often evoked a response from the audience.

To replace the pursuit of purpose with God's promises, you must find a trustworthy friend who can grow, challenge, and hold you on merciless days. We don't need 1,000 followers on social media. We need one friend we can call at 3 a.m. when we're on the bathroom floor. We need one person to say, "I'll be right there," when we call and ask for help.

We need one friend who will talk us through the waves as they come crashing over us. We need one friend we can call from the closet floor as we're lying next to the empty bottle, shame ripping through us like a tornado.

Surrendering is hard. It's not for the faint of heart. But if you want to replace your pursuit of purpose with living each day in the promises of God, then you're going to need a friend or two by your side.

Helpers can take different forms. They can be therapists, pastors, mentors, Bible study groups, spouses, parents, siblings, or friends. Don't discount the people that God placed in your life. But seek wise counsel as you navigate this new road of surrender.

If you don't have that person, seeking a therapist or counselor to help you navigate the pain is essential. I found great solace and strength in therapy. Everyone needs one place where they can be heard. If you're considering it, I encourage you to find a safe place to lay your burdens down.

When we are seen in all our human forms, our hurts, pain, hopes, and dreams matter to the world. In that space, there is hope. There is a purpose. But in that process, we can lose sight of the most important thing: A holy God, walking in the world, fully man, fully divine, dying for us.

That is the most important thing.

As Christians, we give all of ourselves to Him. Each step, moment, heartache, and fear is for His glory, purpose, and love, which is to be shown to the world. When our days on this earth end, that is the point.

A Prayer for Starting Over

Dear Lord,

Today, I pray that Your grace and sacrifice wash over my heart. Please give me the courage to surrender everything into your sovereign hands. Allow me to find strength in your promises. Give me clarity and confidence to see Your hand upon my life. Give me the faith to hold fast to Your promises and lay my pursuit of purpose at Your feet.

Amen.

PART II REFLECTION:

RELEASING THE IDOL OF PURPOSE

RELEASING THE IDOL OF PURPOSE

Guideposts and Reflection

In our pursuit of purpose, we release the questions that plague our minds and hearts. We find a simple, eternal truth that allows us to find the peace of knowing we are forever held in the sovereign Savior's arms. We no longer need to ask, "What is my purpose?" because we have His promises.

God's promises sustain us. We replace our pursuit of purpose with the promises of God's truth.

- We cling to the promise of God's eternal love.
- We survive in the promise of Jesus's resurrection.
- We surrender to the promise of God's never-ending, too-big-to-hold forgiveness.
- We cling to the promise that God created us in His image.
- We cling to the promise that God will never leave us nor forsake us.
- We cling to the promise that despite what we see, God is always bigger.

Chapter 5: How do your perceptions of your identity influence how you consider purpose?

_____

_____

_____

_____

_____

_____

Chapter 6: What areas of your performance or accomplishments affect your understanding of purpose?

_____

_____

_____

_____

_____

_____

_____

_____

Chapter 7: How can you replace the pain of purpose with finding ways to help ease the suffering of others?

_____

_____

_____

_____

_____

_____

_____

Chapter 8: What areas of your life can you surrender and start to find freedom to live in the daily promises of God?

_____

_____

_____

_____

_____

_____

_____

_____

Journal

Spend a few minutes reflecting on each area: *identity, performance, suffering,* and *freedom*, and write a few ways that you hope to lay down the pursuit of purpose and replace it with God's promises in your daily routine:

IDENTITY

_____

_____

_____

_____

_____

PERFORMANCE

_____

_____

_____

_____

_____

_____

SUFFERING

_____

_____

_____

_____

_____

_____

_____

FREEDOM

_____

_____

_____

_____

_____

_____

_____

A Prayer for You

Dear Lord,

Today, I offer my heart into Your sovereign hands. The heart that wants, with desperation, to know that I am living a life fully dedicated to Your purpose and plan. I ask You, Lord, to give me the clarity and wisdom to see when my pursuit of purpose pulls me away from You. Please replace that pursuit with Your promises so I can see your heart in each moment. Thank You for the abundance of blessings You have provided. Let me continue this journey, walking hand in hand with You.

Amen.

PART III: LIVING IN THE PROMISE

EMBRACING A LIFE OF PROMISE

It is the heart that perceives God, and not the reason.

—*Blaise Pascal*

Have you ever tried to count a jar of jellybeans? Maybe you were invited to a baby shower or holiday party, and the host decided to raffle off a coffee mug or spa vacation. You were asked to guess the number of items in the jar. Do you know this game? Jars are filled with safety pins, jellybeans, or red and green M&M's; we gather around, hoping to win the coveted gift certificate or tin of cookies. The person closest to guessing the exact number wins the prize!

No matter how many times I tried, I always lost the game! Over the years, I devised different strategies to calculate the volume in the jar. For example, if I counted the items on the outside, then I could multiply that number by a random factor and guess the answer. Alas, I never won. But I dedicated a lot of time trying to answer the question.

Similarly, scholars and theologians have dedicated copious amounts of time to counting God's promises. Like jellybeans in a very large jar, the number is confusing. It varies depending upon who you ask and ranges from 30,000 to 160. But a consensus estimates there are over 8,810 promises in the Bible, with 7,487 given to humankind.[112] I confess that number is much larger than I would have guessed.

I didn't count them all, but I did some light research.

Finding Promise in the Bible

The word "promise" appears in the Bible in various translations. In general, it's found 163 times.[113] Here are a few examples of how it is translated:

- the word *havtacha* comes from the root word meaning sureness or security
- *epaggelia* means a summons or promise
- *omer* is defined as a promise, speech, thing, or word
- *diathéké* is a testament, will, or covenant

When we talk about the promises of God, we are referring to something that can be *secure: a testament, a will, or a covenant.* So, it's easy to see why counting the number of promises is difficult. Even the words used in Scripture vary. One could get discouraged, but this offers us great hope. If we want to embrace a life of promise, we must first understand the enormous opportunities where we can find them. God's promises are found in all things. But to see them, we must learn to see the depth and hope they provide. We must again learn to ask different questions.

The Hope of His Promise

God's promises are divine and sovereign, unlike those offered by man. R.C. Sproul explains that biblical covenants have elements of promise, but the ones God offers are different. **God alone sets the terms and makes the promise.**[114] Therefore, by His character, God cannot fail to follow through on His promises.

God's promises are obligations that He imposes upon Himself.[115] The biblical covenants are founded on God's divine promise. They are the basis for everything Christianity holds true: redemption, salvation, and grace. Without the promise, none of these are valid.

If we're going to live a life of divine promise, then we must be certain the promise is true. We find that certainty in Hebrews 6:17–18.

> *When God desired to show more convincingly to the heirs of the promise the unchangeable character of his purpose, he guaranteed it with an oath, so that by two unchangeable things, it is impossible for God to lie.*

God cannot lie, so He cannot break His promise to us. In that truth, we find the depth and strength that God's promise offers.

> *We have this as a sure and steadfast anchor of the soul, a hope that enters into the inner place behind the curtain, where Jesus has gone, as a forerunner on our behalf* (v 19–20).

The promises of God are vast. They are the anchors of our souls. Their revelation should offer us great hope, the same that is found in Christ Jesus. God's promises are clear,

THE PROMISES OF GOD ARE VAST. THEY ARE THE ANCHORS OF OUR SOULS.

true, and sovereign. Unlike our understanding and definitions of purpose, God's promises offer clarity for our hearts, minds, and souls.

The Clarity of His Promises

Looking back at our purpose Scriptures, as discussed in Chapter 1, we can compare the difference between purpose and promise. In the purpose verse, we see language like the following:

> *"And we know that for those who love God, all things work together for good, for those who are called according to his **purpose**"* (Romans 8:28).

Despite our confidence in God's sovereignty, this verse leaves us with a degree of ambiguity. It says, "For those who love God, ALL things work together for GOOD for those who are called ACCORDING TO HIS PURPOSE."

We understand that **all things** work together for **good,** according to **His purpose.** That statement gives us hope and a sense of peace, telling us that no matter what happens today, God is sovereign. If we work according to His purpose, He will work everything out.

But it doesn't tell us how to live our daily lives or what to do when things go awry. How do we respond? We must look to other sources of sovereign strength for the answer. We must choose to focus on promises instead of purpose.

God's promises offer greater clarity and hope. Living a life of promise is many things. It's more than clinging to the feet of Jesus. It's living in the confidence and clarity that God's promises are available for us each day. If we commit to living a life of promise over purpose, we cling to His truth. We learn to identify and decipher the promises presented in Scripture or the world. When we do, we can hold onto them with confidence on the days when life gets hard.

The Promise Inventory

I like lists. I have them on my phone and computer, on Post-it notes around my office, car, and even in my purse. I've found that if I'm trying to learn a concept, I must write it down. I need to make a list and post it where I can see it regularly.

So, let's perform a "promise inventory" using Psalm 119 to see the clarity of God's promises. Using it, we will outline examples of how to decipher and identify God's promises and apply them to our daily lives.

Psalm 119: Defining Our Guideposts

Psalm 119 is an acrostic poem. It's the longest chapter in the Bible, with each stanza beginning with the successive letters of the Hebrew alphabet. In it, David captures some of God's promises. Matthew Henry explains that Psalm 119 is a "chest of gold rings." He offers that it seems to be a collection of David's pious and devout writings, "the short and sudden breathings and evaluations of his soul to God, which he wrote down as they occurred."[116]

Psalm 119 is a collection of prayers. It includes prayers of praise, lament, vindication, obedience, and petitions for wisdom.[117] So, in this section of Scripture, we could spend countless hours digging into each element. But that's not the goal of this exercise.

We want to use it as a framework to learn how to study and see the promises in Scripture. But before we look at the promises, remember one principal element: **God gives us guideposts along our daily journey.** He offers us small, daily reminders of who we are and who He is. This allows us to live in the space of letting all of God live through each part of us. Even the painful parts. Even the messy ones.

We can't find God's promises without His Word. And in God's Word, we find His promises laid out before us like gifts waiting to be both revealed and received. The brightest one is listed below:

God's word is a lamp for my feet and a light on my path.[118]

We must use God's Word as our guidepost. Without it, we are lost at sea, floating in the darkness for literal and spiritual eternity. God's Word will light our path. If we use it, His Word will reveal the steps we need to take. Once we commit to using His Word as our guide, we then begin building a framework of promises around our lives. This framework will grow over time just like faith.

So, let's start the first part together!

Tethering to the Promises of God

As we said before, there are over 8,000 promises from God. This study will not exhaust them. But we can find foundational markers or guideposts to pitch our tent, securing our lives to the promises like tethered poles that keep us from blowing back and forth as the seasonal winds of life change.

Do you like to go camping? Serving in the military, we had times when we went to a remote site and pitched a tent or built an antenna that we could use to communicate across the state or region. The large antenna masts had to be connected to guide wires that secured them to the ground.

God's promises are like guidewires. We need to place stakes in the ground and securely fashion our lifelines to each one so we can anchor His Word to our souls.

Here are eight promises, pulled from Psalm 119, to build your base.

Building Your Base

- **Promise 1**: The Lord will fulfill His promises to those who *fear* him (v38).
  - The word "Fear" is *ləyir'āteḵā*, which means reverence or devoted.[119] We must remain humble before the Lord. Not fear in shaking and trembling, but fear in the holy reverence of being both seen and loved by a divine, sovereign God. God is sovereign, not me. I am a vessel. I am fearfully and wonderfully made in His image.
- **Promise 2**: His unfailing love will come to you (v41).
  - God's love never ends. "I have loved you with an everlasting love" (Jeremiah 31:3). The love that God pours out on us never ends. We cling to this promise always.
- **Promise 3**: This is my comfort in my affliction, that your promise gives me *life* (v50).
  - In other translations, this text says, "Thy word has quickened or revived me." God promises to comfort us in our suffering. This is a beautiful intimacy that exchanges despair with hope. God's promise gives us life, and life everlasting. Even when the most painful moments face us and tell us to give up, God gives us life.

- **Promise 4**: He will be gracious to you (v58).

  - As Paul reminds us, God's grace is sufficient for us. It will be enough on grueling and great days. At times, we simply rest on this promise. As a pillar of hope, grace—like love—is a never-ending well where we can return for renewal and rest.

- **Promise 5**: He will sustain you (v116).

  - God will provide the provision we need. This promise gives us the reassurance that, as Jesus said, "Look at the birds of the air: they neither sow nor reap nor gather into barns, and yet your heavenly Father feeds them. Are you not of more value than they?" (Matthew 6:26).

- **Promise 6**: His promises are thoroughly tested (v140).

  - His promises are proven. They are unbreakable.

- **Promise 7**: He will defend your cause and redeem you (v154).

  - God will be your defender. He redeems your name.

- **Promise 8**: He will deliver you from your petitions and requests (v170).

  - God's Word says, "Knock and you shall find. Seek and you shall receive" (Matthew 7:7). Romans tells us that all who ask according to His purpose will receive what is required (Romans 8:28).

These are eight elements to start your promise journey. There are more, and I am confident you'll find them in many places if you look for them. This process takes time, so don't despair. We all stumble. Sometimes, even in our greatest attempts to follow God's promises, we falter. But even then, we can trust that, despite when our eyes fail, His promises remain.[120]

No better story reminds us of how God keeps His promises even when we falter than that of Abraham and Hagar.

God's Promise to Abraham

In the story of Genesis, we learn about the foundational promise God gave to the world. The Lord told Abram to leave his home, country, and people and go to a new land that God would show him.[121] God promised to bless him and make him into a great nation.[122] When Abram arrived in Canaan, the Lord said, "To your offspring, I will give this land."[123] Abram then built an altar to the Lord and continued his journey.

Bruce Waltke, an American Reformed evangelical professor of the Old Testament and Hebrew, explains, "God came to Abram with a promise of great reward, but Abram couldn't see it."[124] Even though Abram had many encounters with God, he still struggled. He traveled to Egypt with his wife, Sarai, and his nephew, Lot. They ran into many challenges.

Abram rescued Lot from destruction, fought kings, offered his wife to Pharaoh, and struggled with many other challenges. But all the while, God held fast to His promise. Eventually, Abram and Sarai began to doubt God. They questioned how the promise would be fulfilled because they couldn't see the plan. They were aging and barren, and the thought that God would give Abram a nation as numerous as the stars in the sky seemed impossible.

An Impossible Promise

Eventually, they took matters into their own hands. In Genesis chapter 16, we are allowed to sit at the kitchen table while Abram and Sarai discuss the promise.

Sarai says, "The Lord has kept me from having children." She is frustrated as she passes the sugar for Abram's coffee. After a few moments, she decides to take matters into her own hands. She offers her slave, Hagar, to Abram.

Sarai says, "Perhaps I can build a family through her."[125]

Silence fills the room.

The Bible is also silent about Abram's words, only telling us that "he agreed."

For many of us, we know how this story ends.

But let's rest here for a moment. If we could pause the screen like on our favorite Netflix series, we'd see Abram standing beside Sarai in their tent surrounded by handmade tapestries and clay pots. They are having a heated discussion. Maybe even an argument.

They believed God's promises so much that they left their homeland, traveled across the desert, fought wars, and survived incineration. Time after time, they walked with God's angels. The Lord Himself walked with Abram.

But they still struggled to see the promise. And in that confusion, they decided to move forward in their own strength. But despite their disbelief and disobedience, God still moved. He upheld His promises. Not only that, but He also chose to invite a slave woman named Hagar to join in His story.

That's our God, friend. His sovereignty covers all. Even amid our weaknesses, His glory is still revealed.

Hagar is one of my favorite women in the Bible because I feel the weight of her pain when I read her story. And it reminds me of how God sees us even in our suffering.

Hagar's Story

As we continue the journey with Abram and Sarai, we meet Hagar. She's Sarai's slave who becomes pregnant against her will. The Bible tells us that during her pregnancy, Sarai mistreated her, and she ran away. But an angel of the Lord found her and said, "Hagar, where have you come from and where are you going?" (Gen 16:8 NIV).

Now, we know the angel knew the answers to both questions. He knew who she was. He knew her story, where she lived, and the challenges she'd faced. And he also knew that God had a purpose to love *her* and to love *the world* through her unplanned pregnancy.

She said, "I'm running away." And the angel told her to go back and submit to her mistress, Sarai.[126] That must have been difficult for Hagar to do. I'm quite certain she had heard about the promises that God offered Abram. She traveled with their family, seeing their challenges. But in her mind, I can only imagine her confusion to see the story unfold in such a manner.

The angel told her, "You will give birth to a son, whose name will be Ishmael. The Lord has heard of your misery."[127]

And at that moment, she named the Lord "*El Roi*," which means "You are the God who sees me." This is the only place in Scripture where this name for God is written.

God told Abram, "I will make your offspring as the dust of the earth, so that if one can count the dust, your offspring also can be counted" (Genesis 13:16). The Lord told Abram to lift his eyes to see the land He would give to him and his offspring. Abram looked up and believed in God.[128]

Hagar, too, realized that the God who created the heavens and the earth saw her at that moment. In all of her pain and hurt, he saw her. And so, she returned and gave birth to a healthy son.

Thirteen years later, God appeared to Abram and said, "I am God Almighty; walk before me faithfully and be blameless. Then I will make my covenant between me and you and will greatly increase your numbers" (Gen. 17:1–2 NIV). Abram was 99 years old and still waiting for the promise.

Waiting for the Promise

I often wonder what happened during those 13 years between when Ishmael was born and God renewed His covenant with Abram. Were there still seasons of doubt for Abram and Sarai? Did Hagar continue to struggle in her role as both slave, wife, and mother? We don't truly know. But, my small understanding of humanity leads me to believe there were days and moments of conflict. I'm sure there were 1,000 arguments about dinner, food, and snide glances or comments projected at her growing belly and the growing boy.

One year later, when Abram turned one hundred, his son Isaac was born. His birth came at the time God had promised (Genesis 21:2). The family celebrated his birth, and after he was weaned, they celebrated again. But Sarah saw Ishmael mocking his little brother as big brothers often do. And she asked Abram to send him and his mother away. Abram asked God for guidance, and God confirmed the request, assuring Abram that He would also make Ishmael into a nation because of his lineage as his son.

So, Hagar again went out into the desert, this time with her son.

And this is where my heart breaks: I consider how she struggled as she walked in the desert with her son, not knowing where she would go or how to care for him. But even in this, God kept His promises.

Redeeming His Promise

After their water supply ran out, Hagar placed him under a tree and walked away because she couldn't bear to watch him die. As she cried, an angel of God called to her and said, "Do not be afraid. God has heard the boy crying. Lift him up and take him by the hand, for I will make him into a great nation" (Gen. 21:17–18). Then her eyes were opened, and she saw the well of water. And so, she gave her son a drink (v.19–20).

Despite her situation or fears, she chose to rise, take him by the hand, and believe in God's promises. She remembered the promise that He saw her, the *El Roi*. She believed the promise that He would provide comfort for her suffering.

SHE BELIEVED THE PROMISE THAT HE WOULD PROVIDE COMFORT FOR HER SUFFERING.

She trusted the promise that He would not leave her and hoped in the promise that her son would be made into a great nation. At that moment, I don't think she cared much about building a legacy but more so about believing her son would grow and be safe. That would have been a great comfort to her.

But those promises were not always clear, even in the desert. They were revealed when she surrendered everything into God's sovereign hands. Trust. Faith. Hope.

The angel instructed her to "take him by the hand," which translates to *"make strong your hand in His."*

We ask, "How do I live a life of promise?"

The answer: Make strong your hand in His.

Like children holding onto the hand of their parents as they cross the busy street or navigate the rocky terrain of a gravel path, they hold tightly to their hands. You must do the same to Him.

Do you pray? *Yes.*

Surrender? *Of course.*

Be obedient? *Absolutely.*

But none of that really matters unless you strengthen your hand in His. You cannot always trust what you see; you must trust in the One who sees you.

The Evidence of Your Eyes

Sixteenth-century philosopher, mathematician, and theologian Blaise Pascal influenced the world of apologetics and Christianity with his writings about the hidden God. Many people in his time contemplated the truth of God's existence. He questioned if the manifestation of God could be seen on earth or if His presence was hidden. He writes:

> *God is not the kind of being who stands at the end of the argument, nor does he want to be ignored. He is intensely passionate and when he comes into a relationship with people, he unites himself with them in the depths of their soul and makes them incapable of having any other end but him.*

Simply put, God wants a relationship with you. But sometimes, seeing that woven through our identities, faith, and the ever-changing world is unpleasant. We must strive to gain a new perspective.

Gaining A New Perspective

At the beginning of our purpose journey together, I offered you two questions:

1) **What would your life be like if you focused on God's promises instead of chasing after purpose?**

2) **How can you live a life where all of God lives through all of you?**

Both are complicated tasks. Having attempted to live my life over the past few years, seeing and holding onto the promises of God is, at times, difficult. But today, I see the futility of chasing after purpose with great clarity. It's as if a veil has been lifted from my eyes, and I can now see the deception and the confusion that quest brought to me and to others.

Each day, as I read God's Word, work through my daily schedule, or listen to a sermon, I find new promises. I started a new You Version devotion for the Advent season today. In it, the writer focuses on the promises of God.

Now, I see them everywhere, and that brings me immense joy. Each time I find the word in the Scriptures or in conversations with others, I am reassured that this path, the promise path, is the one I am called to take. It is the one that continues, time after time, to bring me reassurance and confidence that I am living in the promises of God. And that blessed assurance brings me peace.

I cannot give you a five-step plan for walking with God. But I can offer you a promise path that is proven to give you hope.

We continuously ask, Am I living His will? Am I being a good steward of the time, talents, and treasures that He's given to me?

The answer: walk with Him.

Are your daily choices pointing you back to the Father's heart? The promises will remind you, repeatedly, of His heart. And on that path, you will find peace.

As Pascal reminds us, "God unites himself in the depths of our soul. We can either have this kind of intimate personal encounter with God, or [we] don't have him at all."[129]

The author Graham Tomlin further explains:

> [God] hides himself in creation, and reveals himself in humble, hidden form in a man who goes to a cross, so that those who are idly curious, who don't really want this kind of relationship with God and are only playing theological games, will not find him. Yet those who hunger for him deep within themselves, who are desperate to know him, they and they alone will find what they are looking for.[130]

This reminds us that we, those desperate to know Him, *will* find Him.

Finding Jesus

In a season of drought, I spent time longing for peace. Sitting in my bedroom looking out across the dark forest nestled around my home one night, I heard His voice. He simply said, "Come and find me."

At that moment, I thought that I knew Him already. I knew His voice. I'd seen His face in my heart. But I didn't know that call was for something else. As I sought to walk with Him, I found a depth to Him I had never known.

There are over 8,000 promises that God has given to us. If we are to live each day in the promises of God, we will revisit several of them countless times. Each day is an intentional journey.

In the following three chapters, we'll explore the three common promises that intersect with our pursuit of purpose: *grace, wisdom, and provision.*

- The promise of **grace** offers us confidence instead of condemnation.
- The promise of **wisdom** provides clarity versus confusion.
- The promise of **provision** gives us courage instead of cowardice.

In each of these promises, we find the keys to living "fully alive" in Christ. Through them, we find the daily tools to lay down our purpose anxiety and live in God's peace. So, we'll explore each one, and I'll offer practical ways to walk daily on the promise path.

The Promise Path

The quest for purpose often brings confusion and doubt; it leads to anxiety and an uneasiness that's difficult to describe. But God's promises bring renewal, hope, and peace. God's promises are eternal. Man's promises sometimes falter and fade. In this quest to know God, to seek His face, and to let all of Him live through all of me, I realize now that I need His promises. They are the keys that unlock the questions in my heart and mind.

They are the missing links I've been seeking most of my life. They are, and have always been, my truth.

They are the pillars that keep me grounded on grinding days when the world takes those I love away. When my children face grueling hurt or when I see the wounds that abuse and deception heap into the world, I look for His promises instead of purpose.

And in those moments, His promises give me hope. Jeremiah 29:11 says, "For I know the plans I have for you, declares the Lord. Plans for welfare and not for evil, to give you a future and a hope." We know that verse well. But in verse 10, Jeremiah tells us that the Lord says, "When 70 years are completed for Babylon, I will come to you and fulfill *my good promise* to bring you back to this place."[131]

No matter what stands before us, there is always a promise. And In His promises, I find my hope. My prayer is that you will find it as well.

A Prayer to See His Promises

Dear Lord,

Thank You for revealing Yourself in both intimate and powerful ways. I pray Your promises will be a guidepost to light my path daily so I can see You in all things. Please let Your Word guide me and draw me closer to You.

Amen.

CHOOSING THE CONFIDENCE OF GRACE

> To live by grace means to acknowledge my
> whole life story, the light side and the dark.
>
> —*Brennan Manning*

Thirteen years ago, I started serving in a crisis pregnancy center. My own experiences with unplanned pregnancies at times left me feeling alone and confused. I empathized with women's challenges as I walked through my own story of distrust and doubt. I saw a familiar fear in their eyes as they faced their pregnancy decisions.

A few years into the ministry, I spoke with a woman who loved the Lord. She taught at a Christian school, was married, and had one son she loved beyond measure. One afternoon, she shared her struggles with finding her purpose. Her son was set to graduate from high school, and she was entering the season of transition and unsure of what she should do. I shared my experience while serving in the pregnancy ministry and the hope and encouragement I found each week volunteering at our local center. She asked lots of questions about our roles as client mentors and the programs we offered. Then, she sat silent, looking off into the distance.

After a few moments, I offered to help her find a center close to her home if she wanted to volunteer. I shared how I thought it would be an excellent place for her to help families in this new season of her life. As a Christian school teacher, she loved helping people; it would be a great way to make new friends and grow in her faith.

As we sat for a few minutes, she leaned forward, lowered her voice, and said, "You probably don't know this, but I had an abortion before. Actually, I had five."

The weight of her words hovered like a storm cloud just waiting to erupt.

I sat silent, unsure of what to say.

She continued, "When I was younger, I made decisions that today I regret. I love my son. He is my whole heart. But sometimes, I think God may punish me for my choices. I wait at night, lingering on the edge of my bed, watching to see if God will take my son from me as payment for the sins of my youth."

My heart broke for her. This was a woman who, at the age of eight, ushered her cousin to the Lord's feet, leading her in a salvation prayer so she could commit to following Jesus.

This is the same woman who overcame abuse and divorce and struggled with self-confidence and weight issues for years. She strived to raise her only son to know the Lord. Each day before he left for school, she would pray the Armor of God over him, asking God to protect him and keep him safe.

But despite her love for the Lord, she carried guilt, condemnation, and confusion for years. Every day, she feared the wrath of God.

As she shared her secret, my words dissolved into vapor. I knew nothing could be said to meet her in the magnitude of her pain. Any word I uttered would be meaningless. She believed her choices disqualified her from grace. That belief clouded her judgment. It changed her perspective of her identity and limited her ability to help others. She held onto the lie that God wouldn't keep His promise to love her unconditionally. The weight of her guilt was crushing.

In Galatians 6, Paul explains how we are to help others carry their crushing burdens. Abortion is a crushing burden. No matter our choices, we all find ourselves in moments of regret. But, friend, rest assured that guilt is not a mantle God asks us to carry. No sin is too great for the grace of God.

IF WE ARE TO PLACE GOD'S PROMISES OVER OUR QUEST FOR PURPOSE AND TO LIVE IN THE DAILY PEACE HIS PROMISES OFFER TRULY, THEN WE MUST LAY DOWN THE MANTLE OF GUILT AND TRUST IN THE PROMISE OF GRACE.

If we are to place God's promises over our quest for purpose and to live in the daily peace His promises offer truly, then we must lay down the mantle of guilt and trust in the promise of grace.

The Mantle of Guilt

Brennan Manning was a Korean War veteran and former Franciscan priest who became the best-selling author of over twenty books. He died in 2013, but not before spending years traveling the world as a self-proclaimed "vagabond evangelist."

I first learned about him during a sermon given by our former pastor. For a time, my family attended a small rural Baptist church equipped with wooden pews and a robed choir.

Joining this church was a significant change from our previous routine. Before this, we spent our Wednesday nights and weekends drinking gallons of glorious southern sweet tea and leading worship accompanied by a drum kit and a fog machine.

When God moved us to our new community, we found a small church and joined the congregation. In this season, God allowed me to sit at the feet of a generous, loving pastor as his words washed over me. I learned how to fall in love with the traditions of the Christian faith. The robes, the choir, and the bells ringing became a soothing balm for my wounded soul. The candles, the silence, and the stained-glass windows showed me a different side of the story of His amazing grace.

Our pastor often quoted passages from Brennan Manning's work. Curiously, I picked up a book one day and immediately fell in love with his heart for grace!

In *The Ragamuffin Gospel*, Manning challenges Christians to see that our spirituality often starts with [our] self and not God.[132] Brennan says, "We focus our sights and emphasis on what we do rather than on what God is doing." And in those moments, we experience what he calls "existential guilt" because our eyes are not on God.

Manning encourages us to consider that when "we focus on the belief that we can pull ourselves up by our bootstraps, we are eventually left to stand face to face with the painful truth of our inadequacy and insufficiency."

He reminds us that "our security is shattered in those moments, and our bootstraps are cut. We discover our inability to add even a single inch to our spiritual stature. And that begins a long winter of discontent that eventually flowers into gloom, pessimism, and subtle despair. Because it goes unrecognized, unnoticed, and unchallenged."[133]

In those moments, we focus on what we did or did not do rather than on who God is. We let our fears and despair cloud God's goodness and sovereignty. We get discouraged when we examine our purpose through our past choices. We believe that our faults or failures define us, but that is not the truth found in God's Word.

The beauty of Manning's story is that he struggled. When he writes about the promise of God's grace, it's because he lived it firsthand. For years, he struggled with alcoholism. In his book "All Is Grace," he shares his struggles with being fully human and trying to serve God through broken pieces. Ultimately, he learned the true meaning of grace as he let God's promises seep into the darkest parts of his soul. His writing is raw, vulnerable, and revealing. In the pages of history, you see his heart and his hang-ups.

Guilt is not something God wants us to carry. Looking at our purpose or past, we struggle to see how a holy God could use us for His divine adventure. If we focus on ourselves, then the equation is flawed. Condemnation starts to seep into the broken and tattered places of our hearts and souls.

Digging into the Scriptures, we see countless promises of God's grace. But don't just take my word for it. No other person's life explains the promise of grace better than my friend, the Apostle Paul.

The Promise of Grace

Paul, the Apostle, was a rebel. Do you know this story? He was born "Saul," a Jewish son born in Tarsus, who spent his youth studying the Hebrew Scriptures and oral traditions. He sat at the feet of Gamaliel (Acts 22:3) in Jerusalem (Acts 23:6) and learned the Jewish faith. His propensity for the law was encouraged.

Then Saul became a religious zealot. In Acts, we see the disciple Stephen teaching the Jewish leaders and accusing them of killing the prophets. After that scathing message, the community gets angered. They cast Stephen out of the city and stone him to death (Acts 7:58).

Saul is instrumental in this persecution (Acts 22:4–5; 26:10–11) as he describes later in his writings throughout the New Testament (1 Cor 15:9, Gal 1:13, Phil 3:6, 1 Tim 1:13).

After Stephen's death, Saul continues to breathe threats against the disciples of the Lord (Acts 9:1) and asks if he could bring the disciples to Jerusalem (v2). He petitions the high priest, who agrees and issues Saul a letter outlining his authority.

But on Saul's way to Damascus, God intervenes. A light from heaven appeared, causing Saul to fall to the ground. Acts 9:4 tells us he heard a voice saying, "Saul, Saul, why are you persecuting me?"

This is the moment when everything changes.

It was the voice of the Lord. Others with Saul heard the voice, but they saw no one.

For the next three days, Saul is blind. He can see nothing. He doesn't eat or drink. At the end of the third day, a disciple named Ananias receives a vision from the Lord.

God said, "Rise and go to the house of Judas and look for a man named Saul. He's seen a vision that a man will come in and lay his hands on his eyes so that he might see again" (Acts 9:11–13). "Go, for he is a chosen instrument of mine to carry my name before the Gentiles and kings and the children of Israel" (v15).

And so, Ananias departs, finds Saul, and lays his hands upon his eyes so that he regains his sight. Immediately, Saul gets up, gets baptized, and proclaims Jesus in the synagogues, saying, "He is the Son of God" (v20).

Paul, now known by his Roman name, spends three years in Arabia and Damascus before returning to Jerusalem (Gal 1:17–18). He continues to share the Gospel of Jesus Christ with the world.

But he was not worthy of that calling. Throughout his ministry, Paul often reminded us that he is the least of those who should be found worthy of God's power or grace.

Paul knows he was set apart before he was born, and [God] who called him by his grace was pleased to reveal his Son to him so that he might preach him among the Gentiles (Gal. 1:15).

Paul did nothing to receive the promise of grace. But God provided grace, nonetheless.

Consuming Grace

In Ephesians, Paul writes about the promise of God's grace: *"For by grace, you have been saved through faith. And this is not your own doing; it is the gift of God, not a result of works, so that no one may boast."*[134]

He received the gift. He didn't ask for it. It wasn't because of his willingness to follow Jesus or because, at the time, he had even acknowledged that Jesus was the Son of Man. God joined Paul on the road to Damascus, and then, after a time of isolation and fear, he regained sight and saw how much God loved and forgave him.

But grace isn't just for the chosen few. As we read in Romans 5:2, it is for all. *"And the grace of God has abounded more than sin."*

Grace.

My pastor once explained that "true grace can be offensive." The power of grace, like love, is consuming if we let it pour into the deepest places of our souls. That is a choice you must make.

Choosing the Promise

If we are to embrace a life of promise, we must acknowledge that the pursuit of purpose is not about us. It's not about what we want or need to do for the world. It's not even about what we failed to do.

It's about God's grace—a gift we never earned but which was freely given to those who choose to accept it.

We may not live a life like Paul. Maybe we didn't persecute another religious group. Or maybe we did. Maybe we've had multiple abortions. Maybe we've been unfaithful to our spouses. Maybe we've committed fraud, theft, or even murder.

Maybe. But no action is greater than the promise of God's amazing grace.

Accepting the Gift of Grace

Jesus came to share the Good News. As Manning explains, "The Good News means we can stop lying to ourselves. The sweet sound of amazing grace saves us from the necessity of self-deception."[135]

He reminds us that "we have been given so much. We have been given God in our souls and Christ in our flesh. We have the power to believe where others deny, to hope where others despair, to love where others hurt."[136]

So, if God has given us the gift and promise of grace, why do we struggle so much? Because we let our past overshadow the promise. To live each day in God's promises, we must learn how to manage our mindset and replace our regret so that we can walk in confidence with the Savior.

TO LIVE EACH DAY IN GOD'S PROMISES, WE MUST LEARN HOW TO MANAGE OUR MINDSET AND REPLACE OUR REGRET SO THAT WE CAN WALK IN CONFIDENCE WITH THE SAVIOR.

Manage Your Mindset

Sometimes, people dismiss the idea of God's grace. When they hear that God loves them, they dismiss it almost like it's a sign of vanity. But Paul tells us in 2 Corinthians 6:1 that he did not receive grace in vain.

It was not vanity that forced God to bestow His grace upon Paul. It was not out of guilt nor because God felt bad for him. He was called to be a part of God's plan. God called Paul to share the Good News with the Gentiles. Paul was living a different life with a different plan. God got his attention so His plans could be fulfilled.

Sometimes, God must get our attention. If we're looking for a purpose to be a certain thing or to look a certain way, we might miss God when He shows up. That, friend, would be a shame.

So, you must change your mindset. As we've already discovered on our purpose journey, we incorrectly think or believe a lot about the pursuit of purpose. We have misconceptions about how it should look or feel. But if we are to walk each day in the promises of God, we must face the fact that accepting the promise of grace is a choice.

Will God use something in your past to bring the Good News to the Gentiles of your generation? *Probably.*

But you must be willing to accept the promise of grace. And once you do, you will receive the confidence of knowing that you walk in the power and promise of God. You must accept that some days you will fail. Others, you will soar. And there will be many in-between days that blend in a great marinade we call "life." But grace is always present. And grace, just like love, never ends.

That promise gives us confidence. We strive to trust God and learn not to rely on our own abilities. The promise path points us back to the Father's heart. This is the enduring journey where we seek to allow all of God to live through all of us.

While you strive to live in the promise of grace, remember that your mindset is your most important asset. Other than faith, it will cause you the greatest amount of peace or despair.

Scripture tells us that wine cannot be poured into an old wineskin because it cannot hold the new wine. *"No one puts new wine into an old wineskin. If he does, the wine will burst the skins, and the wine is destroyed, as are the skins. But the new wine is for fresh wineskins"* (Mark 2:22). It simply means that God's spirit will enter a new vessel.

You are made new in Christ Jesus, and that renewal happens every single day. To live a life of divine purpose, you must replace your regret with His amazing grace.

Replace Your Regret

There will be those times when we regret a choice we've made. When we've made difficult choices, our questions about purpose become distorted. We make this whole thing called life about us and fail to see the promise of grace.

We think life is supposed to look a certain way, but it doesn't. It won't. God gives each of us daily provision and guidance. But it comes only after we choose to live under the umbrella of His sovereign love.

In the last chapter, we examined the promises in Psalm 119. We saw how God offers us love. But love and grace go hand in hand, friend. God loves you, and for that reason alone, He freely gives you the promise of grace.

Like all the others, the beauty of this promise is that it comes in an endless supply. Grace doesn't expire. There is no time or condition that God says, "Well, under THIS situation, I cannot extend grace to you." The Savior never says, "Sorry, you'll have to come back later because the grace jar is empty today." Unlike the jellybeans, there is an endless supply.

To live in the daily promises instead of chasing after purpose, we must learn how to replace our regret with the promise of grace. Trust that the Lord is good. Trust that His love covers a multitude of sins. Trust that His grace is everlasting. That way, we will have a renewed perspective when we look at life or the things in our past that we regret.

Just like Saul, our pursuit can blind us. The promises are the light. We must focus each day on the light and let God's grace shine in all those demanding or dark places. We can only do that by walking each day with the Savior.

Walking with the Savior

Grace doesn't give us a license to drive fast down a road. It's also not the approval to sit on the "salvation bus" your entire life, hoping and waiting for everything to be OK and to have a good life. Nothing in Scripture says that we're promised a good life.

But we are promised grace.

So, if you are trying to reconcile this perception about your purpose but are having a conflict when considering past choices and regrets, consider this.

- Do you think God is more concerned with our past or our hearts?
- What happens if we spend all our time focusing on our good and bad choices versus looking at the promise of grace?

Maybe you need to shift your mindset to the things of God and not the things you want/need/desire.

Our hearts are valuable resources and barometers for finding and listening to the human soul. Yes, Jesus was fully human and fully God.

When we stop focusing on the promise of grace, we forget or miss the gift in front of us today. Jesus died so you might live freely and abundantly under His sovereign covering, not because of the good or bad things you did.

So, as we consider the promises of God, what comes next but grace? Consider Paul. How much grief and shame did he carry after his eyes were opened and the blindness that had consumed his life was lifted? How heavy was the weight of his burden and regret? How many nights did he roll around asking the Lord why? Why did you pick me? Why did you save me? Why did you call me? Our holy Bible is filled with book after book from him as we watch his life and ministry unfold.

But did Paul focus on "his" purpose? No. If there is one person who teaches us about the pursuit of purpose, it's Paul. His eyes, passions, and vocations focused on the promise of God's grace. And through that promise, God called him. He guides, teaches, and trains us about how we should go. Paul explains:

For through the law, I died to the law so I might live to God. I have been crucified with Christ. It is no longer I who live, but Christ who lives in me. And the life I now live in the flesh, I live by faith in the Son of God who loved and gave himself for me. I do not nullify the grace of God, for if righteousness were through the law, then Christ died for no purpose (Galatians 2:19–21).

Remember that our identity and purpose cannot be found inside ourselves. God calls us to focus on Him. We find our identity in Christ alone. Through the daily choice of walking with the

Savior, we find the promise that will sustain us in every season and struggle of life.

Living in the Confidence of Grace

We may crash into condemnation when we strive to live in the promise of grace. If we let our choices define us, we will question our calling. We consider that God might be wrong for saving us. But the response to those questions is "no." You are more worthy than diamonds or gold. And God freely gives you His love and grace in endless supply.

Grace, like love, never expires. Regret keeps us from seeing the hope of the future. You cannot live in the promise and look back at the same time. Like Peter, we must fix our eyes on Christ. We must choose to look forward and to seek the promise everyday with intention.

Here are six steps I offer as a guide to help you focus daily on the promise of grace.

Build Confidence in Christ

Each day, you must choose to focus on the promise of grace. You can use these six simple steps to help you on your daily walk: *Reflect, Release, Repent, Reset, Renew,* and *Repeat.* It helps me shift my perspective when I'm having a particularly difficult day seeing the promise of grace, or the condemnation or guilt of my choices and past regrets plague me.

- *Reflect* on your choices. Consider the source of their motivation.
- *Release* your fears, faults, and failures into God's hands.
- *Repent* your rejections of God's instruction.
- *Reset* your perspective. Choose to focus on the promise instead of the past.
- *Renew* your mind and heart through prayer or worship.
- *Repeat* as many times as needed!

It's a simple challenge, like praying without ceasing. Living a life of promise requires us to shift our perspective and strive to walk on the promise path. It's an enduring journey, friend. The promise of grace never ends. You only need to ask, and it shall be given unto you.

Amazing Grace

Today, if you find me on a sunny day (or not paying attention while cleaning my house), I'm invariably singing or humming the latest tune that sticks in my mind. When my husband and I were first married, the singing was a bit overwhelming for him. At one point, he said, "It's like being married to Mary Poppins!" Alas, the birds never join me in song, but I sing nonetheless.

As a little girl, singing was my favorite pastime. My grandmother played the organ. And I'd often visit her, having sleepovers as we lay in her pink country home on the edge of that small Oklahoma town. It was tucked just outside the city limits, with a porch facing the west so you could sit and watch the sunset across the flowing prairies and fields on a warm summer night.

On lazy afternoons, during the summer or weekends when I'd visit, she'd let me sit at her organ and pluck away at the keys. She didn't mind that my fingers found no specific pattern or plan.

One day, she played the song "Amazing Grace" as I sat beside her and sang. We decided to make a recording for my dad. After we recorded the song, I wrapped the cassette tape in a scratch of paper torn from her notepad. I scribbled a message on it, making it a makeshift album cover.

When I got home, I gave it to him. I wanted him to have something so he could remember the sound of my voice. A few months before, our lives turned topsy-turvy again, and we left. I left the tape as a reminder of my love for him on hard days.

I remembered that moment in 2019 when I returned home to prepare for his funeral. I found the scrap of worn paper tucked inside his desk drawer. Memories of his suffering came rushing back to me.

I could see him sitting in the kitchen of my childhood home, eating breakfast one morning shortly after his open-heart surgery. I went home to care for him, helping with hospital visits and medical appointments. One day, I was mindlessly singing as I swept his kitchen floor:

> *Amazing Grace, how sweet the sound*
> *That saved a wretch like me*
> *I once was lost, but now I'm found*
> *Was blind, but now I see*

Lost in the cleaning rhythm, I didn't notice him sitting at the table until I heard his voice. He said, "Sis, are you a wretch?"

I looked up from my broom, paused, thought about the question, and said, "Yes, Daddy. I am."

I caught his gaze as he looked at me with tired eyes and said, "Me too, Sis. Me too."

I knew what he meant. For many years of his life, he made unhealthy choices. In the end, he regretted many of those decisions. But at that moment, he chose grace. He chose to accept the gift that was freely given and never deserved.

In the last years of his life, I watched him carry that confidence as he navigated a difficult road. He carried the promise of grace daily, even as he grieved all his hurts and past mistakes. And that promise gave him the confidence to let God's love pour through his broken pieces.

And in that love, we both found peace.

A Prayer to Accept His Amazing Grace

Dear Lord,

I pray today that You would open my eyes like Paul so I can see the promise of Your amazing grace in my life. Please give me the wisdom to see that Your promises always remain true despite my past or anxiety about my purpose. Please help me to discover new ways to find Your gift of grace in the wind and the rain each day. Renew my heart to feel Your presence and peace. Allow me to stand under the umbrella of Your love all the days of my life.

Amen.

SEEKING THE CLARITY OF WISDOM

Blessed are those who find wisdom, those who gain understanding,
for she is more profitable silver and yields better returns than gold.

—Proverbs 3:13-14 (NIV)

I don't remember much about being young, and that is often the case. Beautiful moments and memories frame my mind, but others are a blank or garbled canvas. At times, I wish I could reach back inside and find the memories, pulling them out like photos in a forgotten box. Then, I could experience the "remember when's" all over again.

But that is not the case.

Defining moments etch our lives and earmark our history. Some of those moments are painful or foolish. Others mark a leap of faith, when we look back and see God's sovereign hand on our lives. But we don't see beauty or life lessons as they occur. As time passes, God provides clarity and divine wisdom to help us understand their importance.

When my children were young, I constructed a series of "Life Lessons" to mark key moments. Over time, the most important lessons received numbers. For example:

- Life Lesson #268 - Don't share your fork with the dog.
- Life Lesson #54 - Be kind to your brother. One day he'll be bigger than you.
- Life Lesson #6 - Fiber is your friend.
- Life Lesson #1 - I will always love you.

As kids often do, they would question how I knew these lessons. I told them the answers were in the "Mommy Book." But as they got older, they turned suspicious. One day, my son said, "You don't have a Mommy Book."

I challenged him by explaining, "Well, I use lots of books. I start with the Bible, add the U.S. Constitution, and finish with anything else that comes my way."

I remember the look on his face as he relented in his logic. But I do often wish for a mommy book. Over the years, I've made many foolish mistakes. Can you relate? In 1 Corinthians 1:25, Paul says, "For the foolishness of God is wiser than men, and the weakness of God is stronger than men." In this passage, he explains that on God's worst day, He's wiser than our human wisdom and strength combined.

As Christians, we're not limited to our own wisdom. We can't rely on our efforts, emotions, or education to gain the wisdom we need to make sound daily decisions. On our best days, we pale in comparison to the Creator. The clarity we seek to live a life of peace and promise rests in the manifold wisdom of God.

The Manifold Wisdom of God

God intends to make His manifold wisdom known to the rulers and authorities in the heavenly realms according to His eternal purpose, which He accomplished in Christ Jesus.[137]

We learn that God's purpose rests in Christ Jesus. As we've already described in previous chapters, we strive to love God and love the world. But we do this so that the manifold wisdom of God is known.

This can only be done through Christ Jesus our Lord. Jesus reveals the wisdom we seek. Paul asks God to give the church the spirit of wisdom and revelation so we may know Him better.

If we are to replace our pursuit of purpose for living in the daily promises of God, we must strive to know Him better. When we invite Him into our heart spaces, allowing God to live through us, we discover the clarity for our lives.

Seeking the Promise of Wisdom

Timothy Keller explains that "wisdom is not only for deep thinkers. It is how you get through daily life." Consider these four areas of your life:

- Physical
- Psychological
- Relational
- Spiritual

Our pursuit of purpose questions link to each of those areas, and we seek wisdom for everything. We search for the answers to our hardest questions.

- What happens when joyless moments come our way?
- What happens when we face cancer or divorce or layoffs?
- How do we navigate life when our children leave this life before us?
- How do we find God's promises during great pain?
- How do we know we are walking in the fullness and provision of God, despite what stands in front of us today?

Life includes tough questions. Proverbs identifies tools to find wisdom in practical, intellectual, moral, and inquiring ways.

But wisdom isn't only about answering those questions. Wisdom gives us instructions for dealing with others. We also receive opportunities to learn and guidelines for righteousness, justice, and equality. It also provides the tools to understand the word of God.

Wisdom is for all people. As Solomon explains, the fear of the Lord is the beginning of knowledge. But knowledge and wisdom, while connected, are different.

Knowledge vs. Wisdom

Like meaning and purpose, knowledge and wisdom have different definitions. Knowledge focuses on the correct understanding of the world and oneself, while wisdom is an acquired skill. The only way Christians increase in wisdom is through the art of godly living.

When we pursue wisdom by fearing the Lord, we are set apart from others. Solomon explains that only wholehearted pursuit yields the knowledge of God. This includes a healthy fear of Him.

The knowledge and wisdom equation mirrors the connection between comfort and suffering. We are set apart from others by holding a holy reverence and fear of the Lord. As we wholeheartedly pursue God, we grow in wisdom.

The Purpose of Wisdom

God gives us wisdom for many reasons, but increasing wisdom isn't just for our personal use. We receive it so that we can help others make wise choices as well.

When we strive to live a life of promise, we must examine our quest for purpose and our desire for wisdom. Have you elevated your quest for finding your purpose above the wisdom of God? We can become so hyper-focused on our hearts' desires that we fail to surrender our lives to the plans of the Lord.

Purpose helps us project ourselves into the future. The unknown future causes great confusion, which brings anxiety, insecurity, doubt, and fear. Our purpose questions come from the large and small areas of our lives combined. Their intersection seems wrapped like a ball of yarn, never seeing where one part starts or stops.

We start by asking, "What is my purpose?" But then, along life's journey, we gather other questions about purpose as the years pass. We revisit the same question when we lose friends, jobs, faith, health, children, dreams, and joy. We don't often see how the "What is my purpose?" question is a collection of many questions wrapped together.

Chapter 1 examined why pursuing purpose is so important to us. We considered these two elements:

1) We need to identify what drives us.

2) We need to bring order to our lives.

When life gets complicated, we struggle to find our personal, hidden treasure that God placed in the world for us. God's wisdom can answer those questions because life is a complex system of divine design.

A System by Divine Design

I've served in various roles supporting the Department of Defense for almost 30 years, focusing a large portion of my efforts in systems engineering and design. In 2016, I attended my first *Design Thinking* course. *Design Thinking* explores an abstract problem to find potential solutions. It includes elements of analysis and systems thinking. One must understand both the elements and the system influencing the environment. In a simple system, it's easy. But as the environment grows more complex, the options for influence are endless.

Consider a bathtub. At its basic level, a bathtub is a simple system with only three parts: the faucet, the tub, and the drain. If there is a problem, it's easy to identify or determine the cause. In a bathtub, water goes in, sits in the tub, and flows out the drain—a simple system.

But with something like the pursuit of purpose, decisions become complex. Like a roadmap, we try to lay our lives flat and decide when to turn left or right. Life is the world's largest chess game. The abstract nature of a complex system is that it doesn't have a specific start or end point. They are not linear, and so the options are endless.

What happens when we add cancer, job loss, or disability? What happens when we have sad stuff in life? Where do those go? There isn't a large "Game of Life" board in the spiritual cosmos that tells each of us when to turn left or right.

Life is too complex for that. Why do we think we can precisely map out the elements of purpose or life? Timothy Keller reminds us that "wisdom often comes through the pain of personal confrontation, from learning from one's mistakes or from the suffering God judiciously allows into our lives. Wisdom is hard-won."

The development of wisdom comes in seasons of hardship. The four areas listed above show how we will struggle daily with each.

- **Physical Needs:** Our need for food, clothing, shelter, protection, and survival
- **Psychological:** Our attempt to relieve the actual or perceived threat of pain
- **Relational:** Our desire to connect with others
- **Spiritual:** The places where God is doing work in us

> **THE ONLY WAY TO LIVE IN PEACE IS TO RELY DAILY ON THE WISDOM OF GOD.**

The only way to live in peace to rely daily on the wisdom of God.

Today, we don't understand how to hear or discern the Spirit. Thus, our desires and needs guide our lives; we no longer understand our true selves. But we're not alone. We see how the desire for wisdom caused humanity's fall.

The Girl in the Garden

Eve, the girl in the garden, also sought answers to perplexing questions. Scripture tells us that the food of the Tree of Knowledge of good and evil was desired to make one wise.

> *It was a delight to the eyes and that the tree was to be desired to make <u>one wise</u>, she took of its fruit and ate and she gave some to her husband* (Genesis 3:6).

And so, Eve ate from the tree.

Wisdom, or the quest for it, isn't evil. We see entire books dedicated to it, including Proverbs and Ecclesiastes. Solomon talks about it at length. He explains how he searched for it and in the end, everything, including wisdom, is futile without God. It is, as Solomon explained, "a chasing after the wind" (Ecclesiastes 2:11).

Interestingly, Eve sought wisdom or insight. Many commentaries explain the deliberate rebellion of Adam and Eve against God. But the promise of wisdom motivated her to eat from the tree. The entire fall of humanity rests on the shoulders of a girl in a garden who wanted to better understand things. And look at what happened—eternal damnation.

If we are to live each day with the promise of wisdom, how do we ensure we do not fall to the same destruction as Eve? How can we live each day with the promise of wisdom without letting the quest consume us? We place our absolute trust in the Lord, surrender to His sovereignty, seek the Spirit, and find rest in Him.

Step 1: Surrender

Have you ever tried to have a productive conversation with a defensive person? Or your teenage or young child who, with all their might, refuses to give you an inch? No matter your diligence, their defensive position is a fortress, and it's impossible to penetrate its exterior. At times, that is the same way we present ourselves to God. We carry layers of armor as if we're planning to launch into battle.

It's not 100% our fault. Throughout our daily lives, we gather many items for protection. We strap on shields in case we get shot by a stray bullet. We carry extra magazines of ammo in case we run low trying to defend our position. We put extra lights in our pockets in case it gets dark. Finally, we stash a small package of Jolly Ranchers candy in our pocket for the moments when we get hungry!

When we arrive at the foot of the cross, we are less like humble servants and more like soldiers preparing for battle. We drop by, asking for wisdom as an afterthought as we run back out into the world.

If we want to receive the wisdom of God, we must drop our weapons. We must submit at the feet of the Father and lay down the shields and barriers we carry. To live in the promises of God, we must surrender and submit all things to God. I know it's entangled and messy. But you're going to have to do it.

If Eve had followed those steps, humanity would have moved along a different path. If she had trusted God, she would have submitted to His authority over her life. If she had asked for guidance, God would have given her more wisdom than she could have ever imagined. But that wasn't in God's sovereign plan.

Step 2: Trust in the Lord

We've discussed God's sovereignty many times. But wisdom does not come on our own accord. We must trust in an unseeable God. That can only be done by listening to the Spirit and learning how to discern its movement.

We may believe that God's ways are higher than ours, but it's difficult to determine the line between human and holy will. We must trust that this purpose paradox makes sense to God.

Over the years, I've often asked this question: How can I know the Father's heart? After many moments of heartache and suffering, I've realized that seeing His heart is a lifetime journey. In each moment where my heart breaks, I rest assured that His does as well.

Step 3: Seek the Spirit

The wind cannot be contained. It is a movement, a whisper. It comes and goes without an introduction or conclusion. But the wind is real like the Spirit is real. It moves without a map or guidebook. You cannot predict it, forecast it. So, you must be able to trust and see that the Spirit is moving of its own accord. Only the Creator knows its place.

John Chapter 1 explains that He [Jesus] was in the beginning with God. All things were made through him, and without him, nothing was made (v3).

Consider this: if the soul sits with God before it is matched with your body, how much does it know? How much can be said about it? What secrets are locked inside?

We strive to live in the image of Christ, but it is God who gave us life. God, through the love of Jesus Christ, offers salvation. But this love and hope are found in the Creator. Jesus gives and brings us life, but not absent the Father.

He does this through the Spirit. By connecting to the Holy Spirit, we hear unknowable words. A connection is made between our soul and God. A deep connection that unlocks the power and wisdom of the Father.

So how do we encourage this connection? How do we draw deeper into the Spirit so that we can open the passageway to our soul? We place our heart and mind at rest.

Step 4: Rest in Him

The posture of our heart and mind must at first be at rest. Waiting. We are waiting for the wind. As John explains, *"The wind blows where it wishes and you hear its sound, but you do not know where it comes from or where it goes. So, it is with everyone who is born of the Spirit"*[138]

We do not know where the wind will come from, but once it moves, we know. Or once we hear it, we know it to be true and present. You cannot chase the wind unless you are a storm chaser. And then you make your whole career out of chasing the wind.

We know that the Spirit of God moves without ceasing. It hovers; it groans. We must trust the Spirit because if we are being pulled by it or pushed by it, we won't always know which way to go.

This is such a deep place of self-reflection, stillness, and oneness with the Father. We listen before talking, moving, and writing. We listen to the Spirit as He calls us. In that surrender, we learn that wisdom comes in many forms. Learning to walk with the Savior is an intentional practice.

Learning to Walk with the Savior

The promise of wisdom is not for our own personal gain. God offers us wisdom so that we may grow in Him. We revisit the promise of wisdom daily in our attempts to decide how we live.

Proverbs 3 instructs us to keep six commands in our hearts. They prolong our lives and bring peace and prosperity.

The Six Commands

1) Do not let mercy, kindness, and truth leave you (v3)

2) Trust in and rely on the Lord with all your heart (v5)

3) In all your ways, know, acknowledge, and recognize Him (v6)

4) Do not be wise in your own eyes; fear the Lord and turn away from evil (v7)

5) Honor the Lord with your wealth (v9)

6) Do not reject the disciple of the Lord (v11)

These six commands can be a general guideline for seeking God's wisdom and clarity for a promise-filled life. We don't often know the path to take, but we can use God's promises as the guidepost for our lives.

Wisdom, like grace, is a never-ending promise. We seek the clarity and confidence to know we are being good stewards of the gifts and treasures God has given us. We try to make sense of the confusion this life wields upon our hearts and those we love.

We seek discipline, discernment, and discretion as we live in the daily promise of wisdom.

Discipline

When we consider discipline, we automatically jump to punishment. Discipline is "the practice of training people to obey rules, or a code of behavior, using punishment to correct disobedience."[139]

But it can also be a branch of knowledge. Take engineering, for example. It's a field of study. Students commit themselves to the training that instructs them on the rules that govern their activity and conduct. We, as Christians, also commit to the field of study to wholeheartedly submit to God's authority and instruction.

Timothy Keller explains that "wisdom comes from a pain of personal confrontation, learning from mistakes, and suffering that God allows in our lives."[140] God disciplines us as a tool to increase our wisdom. We must shift our perspective to see those challenges and confrontations as a form of wisdom and growth.

The second way God develops wisdom is through discernment.

Discernment

Discernment is having the "insight and ability to notice distinctions and shades of differences when others only see a blur."[141] Discernment is a skill developed through biblical wisdom. We seek to apply it to our daily life.

By striving to live in the promise of wisdom, we will recognize when different courses of action are possible. Others may only imagine one or two, but over time, we begin to see options and a depth of impact across various paths.

Paul offers this prayer: *May your love abound more and more in knowledge and depth of insight so that you may be able to discern what is best and may be pure and blameless for the day of Christ* (Philippians 1:9–10).

Discernment allows us to make daily decisions using the wisdom of God as our guidepost.

The final element of wisdom is discretion.

Discretion

The book of Proverbs is a lexicon of lessons for our lives. The purpose, as explained in Chapter 1, is "to know wisdom and instruction" (Proverbs 1:2). We learn that discretion is a key element to obtain God's promise.

Solomon uses the word *"mezimmah"* to instruct the student to seek discretion to guard and preserve. Discretion, unlike discipline or discernment, means *to be wise is to expect problems without falling into either the danger of overconfidence or the paralysis of over caution.*[142] We may know what we need to do but are unable to determine how to accomplish it. Discretion provides that answer.

All three elements are important as we seek to live in the daily promises of God's wisdom each day. As you strive to live each day in the promise of wisdom, consider how each one manifests in your life. Consider how you're employing each in your daily decision-making process.

Our lives are etched with defining moments. Those which earmark our history. We often don't see them at the time they occur. But God promises to give us the clarity and divine wisdom to understand their importance and to impart it on others.

In this quest for purpose, we must strive to see how God's steadfast love and faithfulness bring peace. *Shalom* means that "all is well." Only God's wisdom can bring true peace in our life. We must strive to seek His promises.

Through this process, we learn to see the beauty of creation and God's everlasting wisdom. As we learn more about ourselves, new facets of God's character are revealed.

A Prayer to Humbly Seek God's Wisdom

Dear Lord,

Allow me to listen with Your spirit and see with Your eyes so I may know and understand Your heart. Let me hear the words that have not yet been spoken. Help me seek and share Your wisdom and love with the world. Speak to my heart, Lord, and renew all the parts that are broken, tarnished, or bruised.

Amen.

TRUSTING IN GOD'S PROVISION

I will bless her with abundant provisions.

—Psalm 132:15

D o you carry a deep desire for change? I do. I hold a restlessness that rattles within the depths of my soul. Those like me long to see new sites or to feel the wind blow on their faces as they reach the summit of the newest mountain. We strive to create something new, hoping to find a hidden treasure or to discover a better tomorrow.

We are entrepreneurs, apostles, or self-starters, as they say. We strive to change the world. But that desire is often stuck between a need for control and courage. I'll admit that I stagger somewhere between the two.

To live a promise-filled life, we must acknowledge our deep need for security and the restlessness beneath the surface. Provision comes in many forms and factors. Maybe you grew up living a life of poverty, and the thought of having enough food reminds you of the nights you went to bed hungry as a child. Or maybe you believe that, with a varying economy and global pandemics, you must acquire enough financial resources to outlast any crisis. Maybe you've spent your days building a life of security, only to watch it fade away as time and health dwindle before your eyes.

Provision can mean different things to each of us. But our deep desire to acquire it keeps us distracted. When we ask the "What is my purpose?" question, provision is always a part of that equation, whether we know it or not.

What happens when we think we don't have enough? We develop what psychologists call the "scarcity mindset." Once that happens, the deception is in full swing. To live on the promise path, we must admit our need for provision and shift our perspective so we can cling to the guideposts of God's promises daily.

Overcoming a Scarcity Mindset

What happens to your mind when you think you have too little? That's the question two authors investigated in their book, "*Scarcity: The New Science of Having Less and How it Defines Our Lives.*"[143]

Their research shows how we are led astray when we focus on what is missing.

They examine what happens to our minds when we feel like we have too little and how that shapes our choices and behaviors.[144]

It leads to dissatisfaction and struggle.[145]

The beauty of scarcity is that it is a mindset we can choose to allow or control.[146] The authors explain, "We have a subjective perception of what matters and how much we need to accomplish it."[147]

> IF WE'RE NOT CAREFUL, WE CAN EXPERIENCE A SCARCITY MINDSET WITH EVERYTHING WE VALUE IN OUR LIVES.

Scarcity can apply to any resource. Money is the obvious choice, but what about skills, faith, or relationships? What about time or health? If we're not careful, we can experience a scarcity mindset with everything we value in our lives.

But why do we do that? The authors examined the concept of "tunneling,"[148] where we narrow our visual field and only the object inside the tunnel comes into sharper view.

Imagine you're at work. Your boss rushes through the door, announcing that the computer systems in the data center are overheating and must be shut down to preserve the equipment.

At that moment, your field of view limits you to only a few potential options. You can initiate the shutdown or do nothing and wait. Either choice has consequences. You have "tunnel vision." Anything outside the tunnel is foggy, like a photograph. The outside edges are blurry, and you can only focus on the sharp image in the middle.

When we focus on one thing, we inhibit competing concepts. It's like a mental dam. The tunnel holds back everything else from coming into view. Inhibition is a normal response. It keeps our minds protected. But it can also lead to a belief that no other options exist.

Scarcity allows us to deal with pressing needs, like deadlines or overdue bills. In and of itself, that is not inherently bad, but it inhibits other options. You have to sacrifice something today to accomplish a goal. It could be giving up an afternoon of fun to finish a looming project. It could also be foregoing movie night to pay off your doctor's bill or sacrificing weekends while writing your book.

We make these types of decisions and tradeoffs every single day. But if we are going to lay down our pursuit of purpose and walk in the daily promise of God's provision, then we must surrender our fears to Him. Trusting in God's provision will have a cost. We can only do that when we make trust a key aspect of our lives.

The Guidepost of Provision

The first key to living in the promise of provision is to ensure that we trust God will provide all that we need in His time and because of His great love for us. Trust is essential. We discussed it in previous chapters, but do we fully understand it?

Scientists and academic leaders have defined it. Over time, they've developed a concept called "the Trust Equation." I find it fascinating when we can take a concept like trust or motivation and break it into elements we can measure.

In their assessment, trust includes four elements: credibility, reliability, intimacy, and self-orientation. Each is described below:

- **Credibility** includes the words we speak.
- **Reliability** involves our actions.
- **Intimacy** indicates the safety or security we feel when entrusting someone with something.
- **Self-orientation** implies a person's focus, specifically whether it is on him- or herself or on the other person.

It can be written as an equation, with one variable as the denominator and three variables in the numerator.

$$\frac{\text{Credibility (C)} + \text{Respect (R)} + \text{Intimacy (I)}}{\text{Self-orientation (S)}}$$

If we perceive a person's self-orientation as greater than their credibility, respectability, and intimacy, we will have a negative trust toward them.

Conversely, if we believe they are credible and respected, feel a connection toward them, and their self-orientation is less than those attributes, we will have greater trust in them.

Once we can define the trust recipe, it's easy to identify when ingredients are missing.

It's a lot like cooking.

The Recipe for Trust

Growing up, my mother always made homemade cornbread stuffing for the holidays. After I joined the military and moved away, I called her every year, asking for her recipe. No matter how many times I tried it on my own, I often failed or forgot the amounts of sage or chicken broth required.

My mother knew the right amount, even when she didn't measure it. Everything was added based on taste and time.

Trust is a lot like that. If we are to live in the promise of provision, we must trust God and build our faith in Him. He knows the exact amount we need or when it should come.

When I was a child, I never questioned my mother's recipe. I always trusted that our Thanksgiving meal would include a delicious batch of cornbread stuffing.

The same is true of God. Once we commit to the promised path, we truly trust in the wisdom and provision God provides.

Trusting God

We learned how God made an "everlasting covenant" with Abraham, promising that he would be his God and the God of his descendants (Genesis 17:7). This promise is a foundational element of our faith. In Galatians 3:10–18, Paul affirms that the ministry of Jesus is an outworking of God's commitment to the promise given to Abraham to bring blessing to all the nations and to extend Abraham's family of faith.[149]

Our efforts to trust in Jesus and live righteously will last a lifetime. Like love, our trust in God never ends. It continues to strengthen the more we exercise it, like muscles. Like faith, the more we use it, the stronger it grows.

But the beautiful mystery about trusting God is that we don't hold the responsibility. God does. No human being can ever claim to have initiated a reciprocal relationship with God (Romans 11:15–35).

God initiated the relationship. He started it all. Yes, we have free will. But we could never accept the invitation of salvation if it had not been extended to us first. That invitation is His to control. As we read in Romans, "From him and through him and to him are all things" (Romans 11:36). This verse reminds us that trusting God is our response to His sovereign invitation. He first extended love to us. He first promised to provide for us.

Our responsibility is to accept the invitation and trust in the One who promises to provide. We must be obedient and have faith.

The Obedience of Faith

In Romans 6:1–14, Paul explains how the disciple has been freed from the power of sin and the law so that he or she might become "obedient from the heart," entering into the "obedience of faith" (Romans 1:5), which is the primary goal of Paul's mission and the life that God's salvation gift provides.[150]

But faith is the hard part. This concept is called the Obedience of Faith. It tells us that our obedience responds to God's gift of redemption and reconciliation in Jesus. Faith is fully enabled by God's gift of the [Holy] Spirit.[151] But this act of obedience requires us to stop focusing on ourselves. We must focus on the Lord. We must stop chasing after purpose like it's the end of the finish line and there's a prize.

And we must shift our perspective.

In Romans 12:1, Paul tells us how we are to live the remainder of our lives to God as the reasonable return of gratitude, a return of grace for grace (2 Cor 5:15), having been forgiven so graciously joined with Christ in baptism and given the gift of the Holy Spirit, the believer is both free to serve God in righteousness and bound to live for God because the immensity of God's gift (Romans 6:6–7; 12–14; 18–19, 22).

The new life "in Christ" must produce righteousness in the service of God.

We are called to yield our bodies henceforth as tools into God's hands to do and to bring about what is righteous in His sight. That is often hard to do. It takes faith to move forward into uncharted lands.

A Fabric of Faith

Faith is like a muscle; it grows the more we use it. Its very nature enables us to believe without seeing. When we commit to trusting God's provision in all things, our fabric of faith strengthens and expands. In that strengthening, we find ourselves able to endure harder challenges, seek deeper answers, and trust with greater ease.

When I think about provision, I often consider Joshua as he prepared to lead the army of Israel into the promised land.

In Deuteronomy, we see how the Israelites questioned God's promises. Moses sent spies into Canaan. Ten returned, exclaiming they saw giants in the land. But Joshua and Caleb believed they could overthrow the enemies. In the end, God kept them for many years, and due to their unbelief, none but Joshua and Caleb were allowed to enter the promised land. When Moses passed away, Joshua was called to lead the army.

After Moses died, the Lord called Joshua and said, "You and these people get ready to cross the Jordan River into the land I am about to give to them" (Joshua 1:2 [NIV]).

God told Joshua that, as I was with Moses, so I will be with you: I will never leave you nor forsake you. Be strong and courageous because you will lead these people and inherit the land.

In order to do that, Joshua had to obey the laws Moses gave them: "Do not turn from them. Keep the book of the Law always on your lips. Do not be afraid, for the Lord your God will be with you wherever you go" (Joshua 1:9).

Don't be tricked into believing that you're strong enough to make decisions in your own flesh. Our internal desire for self-preservation guides us. The mind is designed to protect the body at all costs. So, it constantly looks for ways to protect us from pain.

Rick Warren said, "You'll always have a battle." If you are considering a day when your life will be less cluttered, painful, busy, or burdened, think again.

We all have battles to fight; those which are both seen and unseen. Mine may look like shame, ambition, and pride. Yours might be consumed by rage, depression, lust, or forgiveness.

But we all have battles to fight.

Growth is that never-ending endeavor of seeking new things. Innovation, creativity, and courage come from this place. We must balance that desire with finding contentment in the insignificant moments of our day.

The Bible tells us that we must intentionally renew our minds. That also means being intentional about how we compare ourselves to others. There is a fine line between being authentically you, aspiring to grow or develop your craft and calling to become the person God has called and equipped you to become and living a life of peace in Him.

Sometimes, a life crisis or traumatic event occurs and changes us. This is called "Post-

THERE IS A FINE LINE BETWEEN BEING AUTHENTICALLY YOU, ASPIRING TO GROW OR DEVELOP YOUR CRAFT AND CALLING TO BECOME THE PERSON GOD HAS CALLED AND EQUIPPED YOU TO BECOME AND LIVING A LIFE OF PEACE IN HIM.

Traumatic Growth." Adversity can unintentionally change how we understand ourselves, others, and the world. It also changes how we relate to other people. But through this process, we can often recognize new opportunities, priorities, or pathways in life. We develop a greater appreciation for the value of life, we recognize our unique strengths, and our spiritual perspectives grow.

This shift in perspective often comes when we decide to trust in God's timing and love. In this season, we genuinely believe "Thy will be done, Lord."

God's Perfect Timing

The purpose of your life is quite simple. As we've examined, the Bible is clear: to love the Lord with your heart, soul, mind, and strength and love your neighbor as yourself. How that particular action plays out depends upon the space the Lord has given to you, how it grows, and within the context of your unique design.

We continue to refine our patience in all seasons of life and learn how to wait on the Lord. We can only do that when we truly trust that God will provide what is needed for us in the season in which it is required.

Like farming, the fruits of the planting are harvested in due time.

Finding Patience in the Fields

Both of my grandfathers were farmers, as were their fathers before them. When I was a little girl, I remember that one raised cattle, and the other plowed fields. But both relied on the earth and their hands to feed their families.

Patience and provision are paradigms, like suffering and comfort. We seek God's provision for all things: food, shelter, clothing, jobs, faith, healing, and redemption. We ask for healing for friends, for life to grow in our wombs, and for the hurt of depression or anxiety to be relieved. But often, God doesn't answer our prayers in the time or way we seek His answers.

It's like a farmer in a field. Farmers reap what they sow. Farmers are beholden to the wind and the rain. They plant, they tend, they weed, they protect, and they wait. They watch, they study, and they adjust as the land speaks through new growth or weather-beaten remnants.

They live by the promise found in 2 Corinthians 9:10 that says, *"Now he who supplies seed to the sower and bread for food will also supply and increase your store of seed and will enlarge the harvest of your righteousness."*

God will supply the seed to the sower and the bread for the food, increasing your store of seed and enlarging your harvest.

It doesn't tell us that he will give you more things. But the harvest is for your righteousness as you align to God's standards.

The interesting thing about righteousness is that you've already received everything you need in your Spirit. The day you gave your life to Christ, you were deemed righteous in God's eyes, but the practical application of living a righteous life is a lifelong journey.

When we consider the promises and provision of God, we see that all things are made through Christ Jesus. They are placed on this earth for our righteousness, so that we can grow in God. But the growth we seek may be different from what God is seeking.

In this journey, we must remember that we cannot grow weary of doing good, for at the proper time we will reap a harvest if we do not give up (Galatians 6:9).

The exact items we harvest will most often be different from what we seek. If we ask for healing but God doesn't answer, then we must trust that the harvest God has planned for us may look different on earth than it does in heaven.

When we pray for a job but one doesn't come, we must trust in God's timing or that there is something else we must learn, a deeper place where we must trust, or a new opportunity where God is calling us to move, grow, and surrender.

For us to walk daily in the promise of God's provision, we must strive to be like Peter and never take our eyes off Jesus.

The Peter Paradox

When we take our eyes off Jesus, like in our earlier example of Peter in the boat, the damage is two-fold.

- First, we look at our insecurities and insufficiencies and consider that, with only our strengths, we should be able to grow.
- Second, we focus on our circumstances and situations and see, in our flesh, what is happening around us.

Neither of those two things focus on God.

When we consider what others have or lack, we struggle with pride in ourselves and in our self-reliance. This causes us to take our eyes off the promises, especially provision, and place our eyes on the resources or limitations in front of us.

Only by keeping our eyes on Jesus can we walk the promised path.

A Collection of Treasures

My dad was a collector of sorts. Nothing really valuable. He spent the majority of his life working in the Oklahoma oil fields. On his daily excursions, he often came across an old, abandoned barn that had remnants of the past left inside. He'd collect old bottles, keys, and other things he found interesting. Once, he acquired an old violin. He called it his "Stradivarius." Sometimes, when family or friends visited, he'd show it to us. It was broken and old, with the strings tattered and torn. But he always believed that he would restore it one day. Unfortunately, as often happens, that day never came.

When he passed away, we found his office filled with boxes of old things he had collected along life's journey. Keys, rocks, nuts, and bolts. You name it. He had so many things. To the average person, they didn't amount to anything of value, but to him, each one represented a moment or memory he treasured.

Our souls are like that. As we go through life, we collect memories that involve hurt, suffering, shame, and joy. We collect so many, and then, when we sit in Sunday morning service and the pastor mentions finding our purpose, we stumble over all of our pieces laid out on the floor, like Legos waiting for a design plan. Our lives include unmatched models of would-be projects waiting for restoration.

Or, if you're like me, you've organized them. Your proverbial space is aligned with nice little boxes, rows, and rows of organized moments, all cataloged and contained so that you know where everything is perfectly placed, so you don't have to be bothered by them.

Nonetheless, your heart is still weary and searching for the confirmation that God's provision is forever. You are still seeking peace after a long day or week. That's because you're looking through the lens clouded with items God didn't intend for you to carry.

The Lord tells us to "take my yoke upon you." In this challenge, we find the promise He challenges us to "take my yoke upon you and learn from me, for I am gentle and humble in heart, and you will find rest for your souls. For my yoke is easy and my burden is light."

God's promises are light and true.

Proverbs 16:2 tells us to commit our work unto the Lord and our plans will be established. It's a simple framework with two steps.

1) We commit to trust the Lord.
2) God establishes the plan.

It's a simple formula: You place your foot into the water, and God will part the seas. I know it often seems confusing at the time, but it doesn't have to be difficult or filled with anxiety and doubt.

We commit to placing our trust and faith in the provision of God. He alone, through Jesus Christ, establishes our steps.

We commit to developing spiritual intimacy with God so that we can see beyond the tunnel to know that His provision and promises extend far beyond our imagination. He makes a way.

We submit to His authority and timing, praying for wisdom to see how the actions in front of us lead us back to the Father's heart. He gives us rest.

And in this process, we find a rhythm to live out God's purpose.

Friend, the promises of God's provision will consume every area of your life. If you simply decide to surrender and commit your work to the Lord, He *will* provide in His time.

Sometimes, that provision looks like healing or grace. Other times, it looks like courage, faith, or forgiveness. Yes, it can also be money or physical resources, but I've learned that it usually has nothing to do with the physical elements and rests on the heart of the matter. God cares more about our character. And in perseverance, we find hope.

A Prayer to Trust the Promise of Provision

Dear Lord,

Today, I sit and rest in the assurance of Your love and provision. I am unbelievably humbled to be afforded the chance to sit in this place today. For the first time, I'm starting to see how everything is connected. Thank You for providing the provisions to pursue my hopes and dreams through Your divine hand. May You always continue to make a way.

Amen.

A BILLION DIFFERENT WAYS

One's whole life is permeating with the presence of God.

—Tyler Staton, *Pray Like Monks, Live Like Fools*

I sat anxiously in the cardiologist's office, waiting for the nurse to order the EKG. A few months before the appointment, I started experiencing random moments of chest pain. They started at the gym. One day, as I jogged on the treadmill, I felt a sharp pain creep across my chest. At first, I dismissed it. I'm relatively young and didn't consider the possibility that my heart might have a condition of concern. But as I jogged, the pain increased. I slowed down, started walking, and rubbed my chest, hoping it would disappear. A few seconds later, it did. So, I continued walking, finished my workout, and headed home.

A few weeks later, it happened again. While sitting in my living room one night, I felt the same tightening and pinching arrive without warning. Again, I dismissed the urgency of it. But it continued. These short, unpredictable incidents continued at random times and places for a few months. Eventually, I scheduled an appointment with my doctor.

When I met him, he said, "You're young and in good health. So, I don't think you have anything to worry about." I told him how my father and grandmother had both suffered from heart disease and how my father had passed away earlier that year from a sudden heart attack. At the mention of those illnesses, the doctor made a referral.

Two weeks later, I sat in the cardiologist's office, explaining why a relatively young, healthy woman needed a heart consultation.

The cardiologist walked into the office, and the image of Steve Martin streamed across my mind. He had a dazzling smile, bright, kind eyes, glasses, and spiky, disheveled white hair—everything that made me think I'd walked right onto the 1998 *Dirty Rotten Scoundrels* movie set where Steve Martin and Michael Caine try to con a young American heiress out of $50,000.

After a few pleasantries and a quick review of my chart, he asked about my issue. I shared my story and history with him, and he looked at me with mild concern. I told him that my chest had been hurting on and off most of the morning. His eyebrows raised slightly as he said, "OK, let me get the nurse," and reached for the door.

Within moments, she walked in holding a bottle of baby aspirin and a clipboard. He said, "Here," handing me four small pills. "Take all of these and lie down. We will order an EKG and see what's going on."

As the nurse left the room, I looked at him concerned and asked, "Well, you only have one heart, right? I guess I better take care of it."

He smiled with wise eyes and said, "Actually, some people get two! But it's better to be safe than sorry!"

And at that moment, I realized I needed to be kinder to my heart. It has been broken, mended, lost, and abused. It has been ignored, abandoned, and mistrusted. Over the years, I've mistranslated its messages countless times. I didn't heed its warning and attempted to numb its pain with years of empty promises.

That was until I learned that everything I have and all I am lies inside one foundational truth: "God loves me with an everlasting love" (Jeremiah 31:3).

That promise reminds me, even today, that God's love never ends. And for that, I owe Him my eternal gratitude.

A Debt of Gratitude

The debt of gratitude we offer God for the gift of eternal life didn't end at the cross. God set in motion a plan for human beings to receive, understand, and respond to His love in endless ways.

Friend, even when we can't name a purpose, we have a promise—or 8,810—to hold and cling to on impossible days. If we allow those promises to seep into our lives in the darkest and hardest places, we'll see that pursuing purpose might not be the best approach. At the very least, we'll see that our question is incomplete.

At first, our purpose questions seem to be about our hearts, goals, dreams, vision, and future. But are they? Indeed, the world needs Christians to love, serve, grow, stand up for justice, and proclaim the Good News. Indeed, it does.

But asking our purpose questions without including the promises is like asking God for a blessing without seeing the sacrifice. It's like thanking God for forgiveness without seeing the abounding grace offered, with no way to repay it. We quietly dismiss the offering of His heart in our attempt to fulfill our purpose.

As we've discovered, purpose can be elusive, like the wind. As the Scripture says, we do not know where it comes from nor where it goes. But God's promises are eternal. They are never-ending, always present and available to everyone. I found these foundational promises as I worked to unwrap my purpose questions. They are not exhaustive, but they are the elements we most often need when we ask questions about purpose.

Scripture tells us that God will never leave us nor forsake us. We strive to be good stewards of the resources we've been given.

We spend hours striving to align our time, talents, and treasures for the good of the Kingdom while feeling more overwhelmed and frustrated at the end of an exceptionally long day. And as we age or try to navigate daily life's challenges, we become increasingly frustrated with the obscurity of purpose. Sometimes we believe God keeps it from us, holding it back from our grasp. And we fall into bed after a long, exhaustive day and say, "God, what is the point?"

So, what is the alternative answer if pursuing a purpose does not bring peace? It's a journey to discover and walk in the promises of God. It's the embodiment, the inhalation of His Word into our hearts so that we can always find the blessed assurances in Him. No matter what happened yesterday, today, or tomorrow, you can share God's love in a billion different ways.

A Billion Different Ways

Let's now return to the story in the beginning of this book, where I sat around the table one night at a youth group talking with our teens about purpose. Remember, I shared with them two things:

God wants you to love Him with your entire heart, soul, mind, and strength and to love your neighbor as yourself.

You can do that in a billion different ways.

If we're honest, that IS the greatest challenge, isn't it? We encounter many ways where we can "love the world." Throughout our lifetime, we will ask these questions many times:

- What job should I pursue?
- Where should I go to school?
- Should I serve in full-time ministry?
- Can I still serve God and love my family well?
- Should I create or design something new?

The answer varies in each season of your life. At times, the answer may be clear. Other times, the answer is cloudy with a chance of meatballs. But throughout this book, we've learned that we must strive to allow God's promises to guide our path. When we rely on His wisdom, provision, and grace, along with countless other promises, we receive the clarity for how we can love the world through His sovereign grace.

God desires to impart His manifold wisdom into the world through Jesus Christ. And in all things, we strive to live a life where all of God lives through all of us. That, friend, will change in each moment of your life.

If we were to simplify it, our purpose is to proclaim the gospel while helping to ease the suffering of others. We point people back to Jesus as the source for all things.

It's a simple reminder, but every person you see needs Jesus. You've been uniquely and wonderfully made to share His love with the world.

- Does that mean God wants your time? *Yes*
- Does He care about your talents and dreams? *Absolutely*
- Should He be the source of your provision and treasures? *Every single day.*

We like to say these things, but if we are going to live on the promise path, we must take inventory and set our sights on a new course.

Time, Talents, and Treasures

Here is a simple questionnaire to take inventory:

1) Where do you spend your time?

Consider all these things: *Vocation, ministry, attending weekly worship, taking care of your family, spending time with friends or loved ones, self-care, fitness, exercise, prayer.*

2) What are your talents? Or What brings you joy?

Here are a few of my examples: *Writing, organizing, leading, encouraging, teaching, designing, coaching, cleaning, speaking, financial planning, singing, etc.* The list goes on and on!

If it's hard to answer that question, here's a different perspective:

3) What are things that you know? Or, What do people commonly ask you to do?

This is both at your job and in your personal life. If you take the time to make a list, you will often find patterns or themes that emerge.

4) How do you steward your treasures?

Consider where you spend your time and money. But also, how do you relate to others? What relationships do you hold dear? What elements of your faith pull you closer to God? Your answers reveal what you value. They also highlight ways that you can love God and love the world in your unique way.

In 1 Timothy 3–7, Paul told Timothy to stay in Ephesus so he could command certain people not to teach false doctrine.

How hard must it have been to stand in the streets and temples and counter a narrative. We assume the person teaching was someone of authority, so it must have been maddening for Timothy to stand firm.

But in verse 5, Paul gives Timothy a vision. "The goal of this command is love, which comes from a pure heart, a good conscience and a sincere faith."

A Pure Heart.

A Good Conscience.

A Sincere Faith.

I often struggle with this one. I don't always hear the Lord speak nor discern the five-point path He would have me take. It's one of the main reasons I've given up on pursuing my purpose; I realized it was a hopeless endeavor, at least in how I previously approached it. I've changed my perspective, and now I strive to see His promises in all things.

We've learned that a promise is "a legally binding declaration that gives the person to whom it is made a right to expect or to claim the performance or forbearance of a specified act."[152]

But is this quest or pursuit of purpose something God ordained us to carry? Or is it man's interpretation of one more religious and human thing? The very essence of who we are is wrapped up in our interpretation of the meaning of life—or, as Victor Frankel said, "man's quest for meaning." And in this journey, we now see that the promise path brings true joy and peace into our lives. It's time that we choose a new approach.

> AND IN THIS JOURNEY, WE NOW SEE THAT THE PROMISE PATH BRINGS TRUE JOY AND PEACE INTO OUR LIVES. IT'S TIME THAT WE CHOOSE A NEW APPROACH.

A New Approach

I love the Lord. When I close my eyes, I sometimes imagine Jesus standing in the middle of my driveway. We have a long, winding gravel path that leads to the main road. Our home is nestled off the street just a bit, hidden behind a swath of pine trees. From the road, the view is unclear. But as you pull in our driveway and inch down the path, our house comes into view.

When I think about Jesus drawing me near, I see Him just at the edge of the bend. I walk out to meet Him, and He waits for me. As I reach Him, I lay my head upon His chest, just like I used to do with my earthly father. And He waits for me.

I often go back to this image when I feel my faith waver.

In those moments, I ask simple questions:

- Do I still love You, Lord?
- Do I trust You?
- Can I see Your hand at this moment?

And then I strive to see the Father's heart.

Even the disciples who walked with Jesus faltered after His return. Even those who knew the sound of His voice questioned His identity. So, when my faith falters, I am encouraged by those who came before me.

God's wisdom is greater than we can ever understand or imagine. So, if we are called to (1) love God and (2) love the world, how can we truly know that we are living in His purpose?

The answer is the same, friend: *We rely on His promises.*

We replace our purpose questions with His promises. While we've explored several, these are the five that bring the greatest clarity in my pursuit of purpose:

- God promises love
- God guarantees grace
- God gives provision
- God offers comfort
- God extends redemption

We layer the pursuit of purpose with many Christian platitudes to try and better understand. But after we've spent the time pursuing it, trying to catch it and contain it, we often look around at the end of a grueling day and still say, "Lord, what is the point?"

We've spent several chapters of this book talking about all the ways to replace our pursuit of purpose with the promises of God.

Through identity, performance, grace, wisdom, and provision, we see how God's purpose for our life is to (1) love Him and (2) love the world.

I am confident that as you continue on this discovery journey, you will learn new and exciting lessons about God's promises.

But to get to "Part 2" of God's purpose, we must consider how we love the world. This is by far the easiest part, friend!

God told us in His Word to love him first: *Now this is the commandment, 4 "Hear, O Israel: The LORD our God, the LORD is one. 5 You shall love the LORD your God with all your heart, soul, and might"* (Deuteronomy 6:1, 4–5).

Jesus added, *"You shall love your neighbor as yourself."* The Law and the Prophets depend upon this (Matthew 22:39–40).

If the instruction is clear, why do we struggle? Determining purpose is difficult, whether you're a scholar, student, or salesperson.

As Christians, we believe we are chosen, called, and created for His good pleasure. So, if we are chosen, and our glory is also important to God, what should we do about that?

First, nothing.

Second, everything.

We are entrusted with the care and safekeeping of our lives. God ordains our steps, but we choose the path we take. And that choice often leads to confusion and doubt. In the book of Acts, Paul further instructs us on how to consider or see this ordination. He writes, *"Who, having come and having seen the grace of God rejoiced and was exhorting all with the resolute purpose of heart to abide in the Lord"* (Acts 11:23).

In Greek, "resolute" means *parakaleo*, or to personally make a call. It instructs believers to offer evidence that stands up in God's court. The root has legal overtones, but the definition is "to call to or for, to exhort, to encourage."

We are called to one's aid. But we can't do that if we can't hear or understand the voice of God. At each step and moment of our life, we have a choice. We can choose to follow Him or to turn away from God. Both have consequences. But for many of us, we are somewhere in the middle. We don't intentionally try to disobey God. We seek the peace to know we're living the best path for our lives. It's not really a question of "good or bad" but more so a consideration of good, better, or best.

Navigating Good, Better, or Best

Jesus taught us that God desires mercy, not sacrifice. Each of us is called to help ease the suffering of others. How you do that today depends upon your unique sphere of influence.

So, a simple question is: How do you use your time, talents, and treasures?

Some days, it might be working late on a deadline at work because a new product is hitting the market. Other times, it might be donating money to a local family GoFundMe who lost their daughter in a car accident. Or it could be spending a Saturday afternoon lying in the grass with your family designing cloud silhouettes.

None of those things are better or worse than the others. Each has a value, but they cannot truly be compared because they encompass radically different elements of life.

Life is not linear. If we are to live a life where all of God lives through all of us, then we must learn to live and measure success by a different standard.

In God's equation, promises never expire. We can rest assured of that, despite what we see in life.

Purpose in All Things

I have dear friends who are battling stage 4 metastatic breast cancer. On the days their health wavers, they rest. They spend time with their children and family. That is their purpose today: to love God and the world. If we think purpose is only about careers, colleges, or commitments, then we've missed the point.

In those moments, sitting in the treatment chair at the cancer center, God lives through every part of them. Even the messy ones. His love and truth have no greater value for a businesswoman sitting in a board meeting in London than for a single mother trying to raise her children or for a 93-year-old grandmother who is at home praying for her family.

No one role, task, talent, or treasure is greater than the other. Because of sin, we all fall short of the glory of God. Equally, we all have the same purpose to love Him and the world.

Comparison is a great deception. We must strive to seek the daily promises in order to see God's sovereign and guiding hand upon our lives. Only then do we find everlasting peace.

Remember, friend, we are entrusted with the glory of God.[153] Jesus considers you trustworthy to carry His message, like a precious gift. We carry it with honor, not fear. We carry it with reverence, not rebuking. We carry the gospel to those who have heard, received, or believed false teachings.

Jesus came into the world to save sinners, for whom I am the worst.[154] But for that very reason, I was shown mercy so that in me, the worst of sinners, Christ Jesus might display His immense patience as an example for those who would believe in Him and have eternal life.

When you see your identity in God, everything changes.

Consider each area below:

- Faith
- Family
- Friendships
- Finances
- Fitness
- Fun

How does each one change or influence your identity, and what do you believe about your pursuit of purpose?

Again, each of these will change over time. Your responsibility is to inspect each one and seek God's promises to navigate your daily life. And if you get disappointed or frustrated, it's OK.

The Disappointment of Expectation

Our expectations are real because when they don't meet our needs or wants, we lose sight of the ultimate, more significant, greater goal.

Over time, we store all those experiences and regrets deep inside ourselves, and then we wonder why we struggle to see the promises of God each day. It's because we're consumed with the loudness of the world and our thoughts!

In his book *Get Your Life Back,* John Eldridge explains how our souls were not designed to carry the world's weight. We have to let those things go. Souls are finite beings; only God is infinite.

How we translate and store those experiences in our souls will determine how much space or room we have to pursue more of God.

In Romans 12:2, we are instructed, "Do not be conformed to this world, but be transformed by the renewal of your mind, that you may discern the will of God what is good and acceptable and perfect."

But what about our hearts? Our hearts and minds are both essential parts of our life. We must release the thoughts that hold us captive and strive to create space in our hearts where God's wisdom and our faith can grow, move, heal, etc.

When we release the pain of the past, we let go of the weight of disappointment. We surrender our expectations and fears, and then our minds and hearts will renew. Then we start to see that our life here is about something other than finding or pursuing purpose. It's about living each day within the promises of God.

You can't do that if your vessels are cluttered. It's like having a storage unit filled with 40 years of unmet expectations, hurt, pain, and disappointment. In that moment, we believe it is easier to close the door and walk away than to face the reality before us.

Turning Away the Promises of God

In the book of Numbers, Moses writes the story of Israel's journey from Mt. Sinai to the borders of the Promised Land of Canaan. After Israel was freed from slavery in Egypt in 1446 B.C., God gave them the Law. They lived, worked, and sojourned. They ate, laughed, and suffered. As they prepared to leave Sinai, they experienced a series of events that led them to stay in the wilderness for 40 years.

Moses sent spies out into the land of Canaan. They were supposed to go into the land and see if they could discover what God had in store for them. When they returned, they came back with different opinions. Two believed that God had, in fact, given them the land for their possession, as He promised. But the other ten saw the giants in the land. That's all they focused on. They turned away from God's provision.

They voted on whether to proceed into the land. The majority declined to go. After their vote, the Lord was disappointed. Why didn't you obey me? And he decided that because of their disobedience, the people would not enter the Promised Land until those responsible for that decision passed away.

They died, never receiving God's promised gift.

Friend, that is not what God wants for you. In Romans 12:9–13, we learn the marks of a true Christian. It is one who does the following:

- Love others
- Work hard
- Rejoice in confident hope
- Be patient in trouble

- Pray
- Be prepared to help God's people
- Be eager to practice hospitality

You can do those in a billion different ways. Purpose is not about platform or position. Our daily walk with the Savior is a constant, ever-changing ribbon that binds us to Him in all things: in the hurt and in the heart, in the laughter and in the weeping. He is our breath, and we offer that life source to others. Breath by breath, moment by moment, tear after tear. In that rhythm, we are at peace.

If you like checklists like me, you can use this daily checklist if you feel overwhelmed or insecure. On the days when you question your walk with God, remember the list from above. Do you love others? Did you work hard, giving your best to each place you lay your hand? Those are the standards against which we should strive to measure our lives. Those are the gifts we offer the world. And in each moment, we draw nearer to Him.

In Christ Alone

When I was a little girl, our home held much pain. I hid in the bathroom for years, lying on the cold tile floor and waiting for the storms to pass. That cold tile floor became my refuge. It became a safe place where no one could hurt me. After years of working in a crisis outreach ministry, I'm convinced that every person deserves one place where no one will hurt them. We need one safe place to lay our burdens down.

Unfortunately, we don't often get that chance with friends, family, or even our church, if we're honest. And so, for a season, I found comfort on the bathroom floor. I hid from the world until I learned how to walk with my Savior, Jesus, the One who died for me and loves me just as I am. I learned how to see His promises above all else. In those moments, I learned to hear His voice and realized that despite what the world says or does, He loves me with an everlasting love.

In my journey with Christ, I discovered that my purpose was not in the world but in Him alone. If I learned how to walk with Him, clinging to the promises of His eternal love, grace, comfort, wisdom, and provision, I could find the greater peace I desired for my life.

When I laid down my pursuit of purpose and replaced it with His promises, I found the peace of knowing that God was a part of my daily life. And in that knowing, I started to see Him in all things. In all places, with all people. I stopped trying to plan all the steps because I knew that only He knew what would come.

Today, I strive daily to stay as close to Him as possible so that my heartbeat becomes His. He exhales, and I inhale. In that intimate dance, we are one. He is mine, and I am His. And then, my purpose is fulfilled.

It's not about diamonds, gold, revenue reports, or bank accounts. It's not about job titles or addresses. It is about His love flowing through all of my broken pieces. And that flowing love spills onto the world, one drop at a time.

A Prayer for the Outpouring of God's Love

Dear Lord,

May I learn to see Your hand in all things. Through that new perspective, may I always find hope and courage to lay down my fear and embrace Your sovereign promises so that I can share Your amazing love with the world. May my heart always sing Your praises, and may I find eternal rest in Your loving arms.

Amen.

PART III REFLECTION:

PRACTICING PROMISE OVER PURPOSE

PRACTICING PROMISE OVER PURPOSE

Guideposts and Reflection

To live each day in the promises of God, you must discover them in the mundane and everyday experiences. Explore various areas of life where promises can be lived out, such as relationships, work, community, and service.

God's promises are for you, friend. They are the foundation of all that we hold and do. They contain the answers to our deepest needs and desires. When we feel vulnerable and afraid to uncover our life's purpose, we can focus on the promises of God. Instead of asking, "What is my purpose?" we ask these questions:

- How can I take God's promises and allow them to refocus my daily perspectives?
- How can I live fully alive in Christ?

God's promises were made **for you**. They are eternal. Today, allow God's truth to help you shift your focus away from the pursuit of purpose and onto the everlasting promises of God.

The questions below can be used in your daily journal. Let's use the acronym B-E-S-T to remember it!

Action Steps:

1) **B—Be intentional:** Start your day by being intentional, cherishing the present, and focusing on your actions and choices.

2) **E—Embrace promises:** Seek out and embrace God's promises in small, everyday moments.

3) **S—Surrender daily:** Make it a beautiful daily routine to surrender your life to God, acknowledging His loving guidance and unwavering authority.

4) **T—Thank Him:** Cultivate a heart overflowing with gratitude, truly appreciating the blessing and promises that God generously weaves into your life

Consider these questions to help you navigate the difficult spaces of your life:

1) What does your heart need today? Write down the few things that immediately come to mind.

_____

_____

_____

_____

_____

_____

_____

2) Are there areas of your life where you don't believe God's love is sufficient to cover them? Past abuse, work, relationships, etc.?

_____

_____

_____

_____

_____

_____

3) Have you hidden "heart spaces" from God's love? If so, what are they?

_____

_____

_____

_____

_____

_____

_____

4) Why do you think these heart spaces are off-limits?

_____

_____

_____

_____

_____

_____

_____

5) How can your perspective of God's promises change your perspective of your purpose?

_____

_____

_____

_____

_____

_____

_____

Journal

Reflection: The Heart Knows - Reframing Your Perspective

Read Jeremiah 31:1–3 and consider how the promise of God's everlasting love applies to you today:

"At the time," declares the Lord, "I will be the God of all the clans of Israel, and they shall be my people." thus says the Lord, "the people who survived the sword found grace in the wilderness; when Israel sought for rest, the Lord appeared to him from far away. I have loved you with an everlasting love; therefore, I have continued my faithfulness to you."

_____

_____

_____

_____

_____

_____

_____

_____

_____

_____

_____

Prayer:

Dear Lord,

Here is my heart. I offer it to You. It is messy, worn, tattered, and bruised. It's been covered by life's moments, and I can't seem to hear it anymore. Please help me to see the promise of Your love today. Can You open a small window of my soul and show me the hidden treasures so I can replace the world's lies with Your love? When I struggle to lay down my control, please help me to see Your love as a promise I can trust. Please help me return my focus to You.

Amen.

AFTERWORD: GROWING IN GOD'S PROMISES

Over the years, I've tried to tend a garden. I start with the best of intentions, planting seedlings and labeling each row in perfect Excel spreadsheet fashion. I love straight lines! I envision a beautiful "secret garden" filled with flowering vines of blossoms and bounty. On early morning walks, I dream of enjoying the sweetness of spring, inhaling the scent of honeysuckle as I meander through its landscape.

But after I've planted the green plants, I return to my busy life, and the weeds begin to grow.

Weeding in a new garden is arduous. It's easier when the plants are established. Their stocks are solid and robust. Budding fruit or flowers bloom on the plants, and you can see the "fruit of your labors," as they say.

But when a seedling first sprouts, it shoots up from the dark soil, and a small, thin blade of green life emerges. That small blade looks a lot like a weed. When tending your garden in those first few weeks, you must be careful not to pluck the seedlings out with the weeds.

If you don't know they are seedlings, you might need clarification. You look at this green thing and ask, "Is that a weed, or is that my cucumber plant?" If you're not sure, you wait. You water, fertilize, and watch as this newfound plant becomes the start of something beautiful. If you're not careful or get in a rush, you might accidentally pull out the new seedling with the weed, not understanding what you see.

If you visited my home today, you'd find pots with overgrown plants. In our compost bin, two scraggly tomato plants sprouted from the seeds of discarded, rotting tomatoes. The plants, left to their own accord, grew across the ground. In a mass of gnarled confusion, they create a great tomato tangle.

And I've left them alone. No fruit grew because the plants were left far too long, and now, only vines and sprawling limbs remain.

Growing with God mimics gardening. We live in a constant state of reflection. We see something and try to discern its value. Is this a weed, or is it the start of something beautiful?

We discover the answers when we examine it through God's holy lens. Only then can we see if the bud is the start of something new. Is it about God or focused on ourselves? Should we remove it or let it remain?

Replacing your pursuit of purpose with living in God's promises is an enduring journey. At times, it might seem difficult. You may find yourself looking at a small sprout and trying to discern if it's the start of something beautiful or if you should pluck it out by its roots. I cannot tell you which one will be for you. But I do know this is part of the process. If our lives are left on autopilot, they will grow into a mass of gnarled confusion like an unkempt garden. And so, we must intentionally tend the ground. We must strive to continue to grow each day in the promises of God.

Each moment in your life is relevant. In every moment, God is with us. Often, I think He's like the woman at the well. He's simply there. Sitting. Waiting for us to come with our arms aching because we're tired of physically carrying the weight of life-giving water and the metaphorical weight of the life we carry. He's there, waiting for us to draw water so we can live and survive. And at that moment, which looks human and unnecessary for a divine Savior, He sees us. He's not asking us for anything but to just sit and rest for a while.

We make purpose about many other things —titles, platforms, etc. But the promise is a gentle whisper. It's the confidence that comes when you're wrapped in the arms of your Savior. It's the gentle whisper we hear in 2 Kings 19. "I am not in the wind," the Lord says, "I am in the whisper."

"Come and find me," the Lord said to me. And I tried to follow, seeking Him in lost and dark spaces, laying down my perceptions and unmet expectations so that I could allow His Spirit and sweet aroma to seep into the deepest pores of my soul.

In the beginning, I thought this book would be a tool to equip the daughters of Christ to live a powerful, spirit-led life. But it became more about finding God's promises in each moment of every day. I discovered how to see the Father's heart and to let all of Him live through all of me.

Our Personal Journey

In 2023, while writing this book, our family lost four family members who were dearly loved. As one imagines, it was a year of significant loss. Each week, I sought to write the pages of this story and lived inside my own purpose storm. I can say, without regret, that the promises of God sustained me on those heart-wrenching and humble days.

In the summer of 2024, my dear friend April, went to live in heaven with Jesus after fighting a five-year war with metastatic breast cancer. As we prepared for her final days, I clung to the promises of God. Some offered purpose as the course in which we should pursue in our Christian life, but I came back to His promises.

The quest to place promise over purpose will be a lifelong journey for each of us. I pray, dear friend, that you found rest here. I pray the words on these pages pull you closer into a sovereign love affair with the One who knows, sees, and loves you —always and forever.

As God said, *I have loved you with an everlasting love.*

Today, I pray you strive to stand in the strength of God's promises before the world pushes them away.

A Fond Farewell

We started this journey by asking a simple yet complex question: *What is my purpose?* We dove into the great abyss of the Christian pursuit of purpose, explored the mantle of Christ and sought to learn how our perspective change when we pick up the cross and say, "Yes, Lord, I will follow You. I will follow You with all that I have. I will give You all my life: my heart, mind, soul, and strength. And I will strive to offer all of You to the world for as much as my human frailty can muster."

We strive to arrive at the place in our lives, on this side of eternity, where we can say that we gave everything to Him with all our being. We attempt to lay down all of ourselves, unwrap every hidden secret, vessel, and deep place inside our hearts that He already knows and loves.

If we're honest, the intimacy of that is appalling. No other human, not even the children that grow within our wombs, has that much intimacy with who we are. No one else has ever touched our soul and held it in their hands. Only God, the Creator, can say who we are and what He has called us to do.

Remember that!

Safe travels, my friend. May you find confidence and peace in the promises of God's everlasting love.

If you'd like to stay connected, I'll share more about my adventures through the pursuit of purpose and unveiling the promises of God on my website.

Visit www.danitacummins.com for the latest updates.

All my love,

Danita

Promise Over Purpose

ACKNOWLEDGMENTS

It truly takes a village, and I've experienced that blessing firsthand. The mentorship, inspiration, and grace extended by my "book tribe" forever changed my life. As each person poured out their hearts, in small or sacrificial ways, I moved from sitting on the floor surrounded by garbled words on scratch paper to holding God's promises in my hand. The magnitude of that offering can never be measured.

My husband, Mark, remains my greatest confidant, partner and friend. Thank you for every moment. May they always see His love in you. Mitchell, Brianna, Wesley, Alyssa, and Gavin, your endless hugs and encouragement are my greatest source of strength. You are my entire heart. I pray that your lives will be filled with the whole measure of His amazing love. Thank you for helping me be brave enough to try, loving me despite my faults, and giving me the honor of being your mom (and mom-in-law).

To Mom and Dad, thank you for loving me without boundaries or limits. To Mom Liz, your heart inspires me. I love each of you more than words could ever say.

Carrie Daws, my first real-life writer friend, your teacher's heart is evident in everything you do. Ten years ago, you converted a corner coffee shop into a writing classroom, forever changing my life. May God keep you forever in His loving arms.

To my gallant beta readers, your willingness to dive into the pages of my first manuscript humbled me beyond words. Jen, Liz, Christina, and Janelle are my anchors. My heart is forever thankful for you.

Sarah Farish and Brenda Covert, your insight, keen eyes, and encouraging hearts made this project more than mere words on paper. You both brought an idea to life, and I am eternally grateful for your book coaching and editing genius. But more so, I'm thankful for your friendship and support.

To Alli Worthington, thank you for your tender nudges, transparent leadership, and hours of afternoon reassurance. Thanks for holding space for me. Thank you and Lisa Whittle for your bold courage in creating Called Creatives Publishing and for giving a new girl like me a seat at the table. Thank you for holding the mantle for us. Steph Meyer Kingery, thank you for your project management and guidance behind the scenes. Thanks for keeping all the trains running on time!

To the Alpha Life team, your prayers, insights, parking lot theology lessons, hugs, infectious laughter, and reassuring words increase my faith in Him. Your unwavering support shows me different facets of the Father's heart daily. Thank you for holding space for those who can't speak for themselves and always pointing me back to the Father's love.

Pastor Gerald "Marv" Gordner, your willingness to answer telephone calls, offer wisdom, and hold space for my faith is humbling. I am thankful for Kim and your loving church family, who continue to punch above their weight class.

To the Called Creatives crew, your presence is a catalyst for seeking greater truth. Your commitment to sharing His story with the world inspires me. Thank you for your unwavering support, endless laughter, late-night pizza parties, and heartfelt prayers.

To countless family and friends, May God bless and keep you, guiding you to greater heights in all your endeavors. But most importantly, may you always seek His promises. May the world forever see His face. May you strive to live a life where all of God lives through all of you.

ENDNOTES

1 I have seen this quote attributed to various sources, including Dr. Martin Luther and also General Robert E. Lee. I am unable to confirm either source.

2 Jeremiah 31:3 (English Standard Version).

3 Compton, William C, and Edward Hoffman. *Positive Psychology: The Science of Happiness and Flourishing.* Thousand Oaks, California: Sage Publications, Inc., 2020, 1.

4 Shephard, Ben. *A War of Nerves: Soldiers and Psychiatrists in the Twentieth Century.* Cambridge: Harvard University Press, 2001, 332.

5 Rainey, Larissa. *The Search for Purpose in Life: An Exploration of Purpose, the Search Process, and Purpose Anxiety,* 2014, 12.

6 Orwell, George. *1984.* London: Secker & Warburg, 1949.

7 "Definition of PARADOX." Merriam-Webster: America's Most Trusted Dictionary. Last modified November 26, 2023. https://www.merriam-webster.com/dictionary/paradox.

8 Frankl, Viktor E. *Man's Search for Meaning.* Washington Square Press, Boston, MA. 1959.

9 Ibid.

10 Ibid.

11 Accessed February 21, 2024. chrome-extension://
efaidnbmnnnibpcajpcglclefindmkaj/https://www.
templeton.org/wp-content/uploads/2020/02/
Psychology-of-Purpose.pdf.

12 "Definition of PURPOSE." Merriam-Webster: America's
Most Trusted Dictionary. Last modified October 20,
2023. https://www.merriam-webster.com/dictionary/
purpose.

13 "Purpose Definition | What Is Purpose." Greater Good.
Accessed February 21, 2024. https://greatergood.berkeley.
edu/topic/purpose/definition

14 The Psychology of Purpose. John Templeton Foundation.
Accessed February 21, 2024. chrome-extension://
efaidnbmnnnibpcajpcglclefindmkaj/https://www.
templeton.org/wp-content/uploads/2020/02/
Psychology-of-Purpose.pdf, 4.

15 *The Psychology of Purpose*. John Templeton Foundation.
Accessed February 21, 2024, 6.

16 Rainey. *The Search for Purpose in Life*.

17 "Bible Gateway Passage: Romans 8:28 -
English Standard Version." Bible Gateway.
Accessed February 22, 2024. https://www.
biblegateway.com/passage/?search=romans%20
8%3A28&version=ESV#fen-ESV-28129a.

18 "Strong's Greek: 4286. πρόθεσις (prothesis) -- 12
Occurrences." Bible Hub: Search, Read, Study the Bible
in Many Languages. Accessed February 22, 2024. https://
biblehub.com/greek/strongs_4286.htm.

19 Genesis 1:27.

20 Ephesians 5:27.

21 Ephesians 2:10.

22 Matthew 28:16-20.

23 Matthew 22:37-40

24 Matthew 22:37-39.

25 Ibid.

26 Matthew 14:22–31.

27 *The Psychology of Purpose.* John Templeton Foundation. Accessed February 21, 2024, 1.

28 Keyes, C.L.M. "Authentic purpose: The spiritual infrastructure of life." *Journal of Management, Spirituality and Religion*, 8(4). 2001, 281-297.

29 Kashdan, T. B., & McKnight, P. E. (2009). Origins of purpose in life: Refining our understanding of a life well lived. *Psychology Topics*, 18(2), 303–316.

30 Ibid, 304.

31 "How to Seek Purpose with Less Anxiety." *Psychology Today.* Accessed February 22, 2024. https://www. psychologytoday.com/us/blog/tracking-wonder/201712/how-seek-purpose-less-anxiety.

32 Cunff, Anne-Laure L. "Purpose Anxiety: The Fear of Not Knowing Your Purpose in Life." Ness Labs. Last modified February 16, 2023. https://nesslabs.com/purpose-anxiety.

33 Rainey, Larissa. (2014). "The Search for Purpose in Life: An Exploration of Purpose, the Search Process, and Purpose Anxiety."

34 Ibid, 50.

35 Kassin, Saul, et al. *Social Psychology.* 10th ed., CenGage Learning, Boston MA. 2017, 56.

36 Ibid., 57.

37 Ibid., 58.

38 Ibid., 80.

39 Rainey, The Search for Purpose in Life, 2.

40 Rainey, The Search for Purpose in Life, 7.

41 Matthew 11:5-25

42 Matthew 11:27

43 Deuteronomy 6:4–6

44 Deuteronomy 7:6-7

45 Deut. 7:9

46 1 Corinthians 8:6 (The Living Bible – TLB)

47 Moberly, R.W.L. (2013). "Old Testament Theology:Reading the Hebrew Bible as Christian Scripture." BakerAcademic:Grand Rapids, MI. p. 8.

48 Ibid, p. 9.

49 Ibid, p.11.

50 Ibid, p. 11

51 Ephesians 3:6-12

52 Hebrews 6:17.

53 "Greek Concordance: βουλῆς (boulēs) -- 1 Occurrence." Bible Hub: Search, Read, Study the Bible in Many Languages. Accessed February 22, 2024. https://biblehub.com/greek/boule_s_1012.htm.

54 Genesis 26:4.

55 Women's ESV Study Bible, Introduction to Genesis. Crossway, Wheaton, IL. 2020, 8.

56 Romans 4:13–15 (The Message).

57 Romans 4:16.

58 Hebrews 6:19.

59 Romans 5:3–5.

60 Tozer, A.W. *A Cloud by Day, a Fire by Night: Finding and Following God's Will for You*. Ada: Baker Books, 2019.

61 2 Corinthians 5:17.

62 Benner, David G. *The Gift of Being Yourself: The Sacred Call to Self-Discovery*. Downers Grove, Illinois: Ivp Books, 2015, 25.

63 Mullainathan, Sendhil, and Eldar Shafir. *Scarcity: The New Science of Having Less and How It Defines Our Lives*. London: Picador, 2014, 12.

64 Genesis 3:1 (New International Version).

65 1 John 4:19.

66 "Prayers Bu St. Augustine of Hippo." Servants of the Pierced Hearts of Jesus and Mary. Accessed February 23, 2024. https://www.piercedhearts.org/theology_heart/wisdom_heart/augustine_prayers.htm.

67 Taylor, Barbara B. Learning to Walk in the Dark. New York: HarperCollins, 2014, 84.

68 Proverbs 23:7 (American Standard Version).

69 Lewis, C. S. *The Problem of Pain*. Grand Rapids: Zondervan, 2001, 654.

70 Eldredge, John. *Get Your Life Back: Everyday Practices for a World Gone Mad*. Nashville: Thomas Nelson, 2020, 24.

71 Matthew 11:29

72 Ibid., 68.

73 "One Third of Your Life is Spent at Work." Gettysburg College. Accessed February 27, 2024. https://www.gettysburg.edu/news/stories?id=79db7b34-630c-4f49-ad32-4ab9ea48e72b#:~:text=The%20average%20person%20will%20spend%2090%2C000%20hours%20at%20work%20over%20a%20lifetime.

74 "Mark D. Roberts: Books, Biography, Latest Update." Amazon.com. Accessed February 28, 2024. https://www.amazon.com/stores/author/B001JS0ZMA/about.

75 Roberts, Mark. "Give Yourself Fully to the Work of the Lord." De Pree Center. Last modified July 11, 2023. https://depree.org/give-yourself-fully-to-the-work-of-the-lord/.

76 Ibid

77 "Maslow's Hierarchy of Needs." Wikipedia, the Free Encyclopedia. Last modified September 19, 2023. https://en.wikipedia.org/wiki/Maslow%27s_hierarchy_of_needs.

78 "Maslow's Hierarchy of Needs." Simply Psychology. Last modified November 3, 2022. https://simplypsychology.org/maslow.html.

79 Maslow's Hierarchy of Needs. Retrieved from https://www.simplypsychology.org/maslow.html

80 Lysova, E., Fletcher, L. Baroudi, S. (2023) What makes work meaningful? Harvard Business Review. Retrieved from https://hbr.org/2023/07/what-makes-work-meaningful

81 C. Bailey and A. Madden, "Time Reclaimed: Temporality and the Experience of Meaningful Work," Work, Employment, & Society (October 2015), doi: 10.1177/0950017015604100.

82 Miller, Darrow. "Work and Worship Blend in One Hebrew Word." Darrow Miller and Friends. Last modified June 21, 2018. https://darrowmillerandfriends.com/2018/07/23/work-worship-go-together/#:~:text=Avodah%20is%20used%20289%20times,(avodah)%20the%20ground.%E2%80%9D.

83 Proverbs 31:16–18.

84 Sloten, John V. *Every Job a Parable: What Walmart Greeters, Nurses, and Astronauts Tell Us about God.* Colorado Springs: NavPress, 2017.

85 Ibid., 5.

86 "Legalism Vs. Gospel Religion by Burk Parsons." Ligonier Ministries. Accessed February 28, 2024. https://www.ligonier.org/learn/articles/legalism-vs-gospel-religion.

87 Crosby, Stephen. *The Silent Killers of the Faith: Overcoming Legalism and Performance Based Religion.* Shippensburg: Destiny Image Publishers, 2005, 12.

88 Ibid., 87.

89 Ibid., 24.

90 Ibid., 15.

91 Ibid., 26.

92 "What Are the Five Heavenly Crowns That Believers Can Receive in Heaven?" GotQuestions.org. Accessed February 28, 2024. https://www.gotquestions.org/heavenly-crowns.html.

93 Swindoll, Charles R. *Insights on Revelation.* Carol Stream: Tyndale House, 2013.

94 Crosby, *The Silent Killers of Faith.*

95 Ecclesiastes 3:11

96 James 1:2.

97 Exodus 3:4-10

98 "Theology Thursday: Storing Treasure in Heaven." GCU. Last modified September 16, 2019. https://www.gcu. edu/blog/theology-ministry/theology-thursday-storing-treasure-heaven.

99 Psalm 139:13.

100 Isaiah 43:1.

101 Matthew 7:7

102 Duckworth, Angela. *Grit: The Power of Passion and Perseverance*. New York: Simon & Schuster, 2016.

103 Eger, Edith E. *The Gift: 14 Lessons to Save Your Life*. New York: Scribner, 2020, 3.

104 Ibid.

105 Ibid., 6.

106 Ibid.

107 1 Corinthians 3:13.

108 Eger, *The Gift*, 9.

109 Raynor, Jordan. *Redeeming Your Time: 7 Biblical Principles for Being Purposeful, Present, and Wildly Productive*. WaterBrook, 2021.

110 Luke 12:17.

111 Ephesians 2:8, "For it is by grace that you have been saved, through faith."

112 Pepperdine Digital Commons | Pepperdine University Research. Accessed February 28, 2024. https://digitalcommons.pepperdine.edu/cgi/viewcontent.cgi?article=1769&context=leaven#:~:text=a%20task%20which%20took%20him,made%

113 "BibleGateway - Keyword Search: Promise." BibleGateway.com: A Searchable Online Bible in over 150 Versions and 50 Languages. Accessed February 28, 2024. https://www.biblegateway.com/quicksearch/?quicksearch=promise&version=ESV.

114 Sproul, R. C. *The Promises of God: Discovering the One Who Keeps His Word*. Colorado Springs, CO: David C Cook, 2013, 1.

115 Ibid.

116 "Commentary on Psalms 119 by Matthew Henry." Blue Letter Bible. Accessed February 28, 2024. https://www.blueletterbible.org/Comm/mhc/Psa/Psa_119.cfm.

117 Ibid.

118 Psalm 119:105.

119 "Hebrew Concordance: Lə·yir·'Ā·ṭe·ḵā -- 1 Occurrence." n.d. Biblehub.com. Accessed February 14, 2024. https://biblehub.com/hebrew/leyiratecha_3374.htm.

120 Psalm 119:123.

121 Genesis 12:1 NIV.

122 Genesis 12:2-3.

123 Genesis 12:7 NIV.

124 Waltke, Bruce K, and Charles Yu. 2007. *An Old Testament Theology: An Exegetical, Canonical, and Thematic Approach*. Grand Rapids, Mich.: Zondervan, 333.

125 Genesis 16:2 (NIV).

126 Genesis 16:9.

127 Genesis 16:11.

128 Waltke, Bruce K. *An Old Testament Theology: An Exegetical, Canonical, and Thematic Approach.* Zondervan Academic, 2011.

129 "Profiles in Faith: Blaise Pascal." n.d. C.S. Lewis Institute. Accessed February 14, 2024. https://www.cslewisinstitute. org/resources/profiles-in-faith-blaise-pascal/.

130 Ibid.

131 Jeremiah 29:10–11.

132 Manning, Brennan. *The Ragamuffin Gospel.* Colorado Springs, Colorado Multnomah Books, 2015, 17.

133 Ibid., 18.

134 Ephesians 2:8-9.

135 Ibid., 23.

136 Ibid., 25.

137 Ephesians 3:10

138 John 3:8.

139 "Definition of DISCIPLINE." Merriam-Webster: America's Most Trusted Dictionary. Last modified September 15, 2023. https://www.merriam-webster.com/ dictionary/discipline.

140 Keller, Timothy, and Kathy Keller. 2017. *God's Wisdom for Navigating Life: A Year of Daily Devotions in the Book of Proverbs.* New York, New York: Viking, 3.

141 Ibid., 4.

142 Keller, *God's Wisdom for Navigating Life,* 5.

143 Mullainathan, Sendhil, and Eldar Shafir. *Scarcity: The New Science of Having Less and How It Defines Our Lives.* London: Picador, 2014.

144 Ibid., 11.

145 Ibid. 11

146 Ibid., 12.

147 Ibid., 11.

148 Ibid., 13.

149 DeSilva, David A. *An Introduction to the New Testament: Contexts, Methods & Ministry Formation.* Downers Grove: InterVarsity Press, 2018, 543.

150 Ibid., 545.

151 Ibid., 548.

152 "Definition of PROMISE." Merriam-Webster: America's Most Trusted Dictionary. Last modified October 2, 2023. https://www.merriam-webster.com/dictionary/promise.

153 1 Timothy 1:11

154 1 Timothy 1:15-17 New Century Version (NCV)

New episodes release the 1st and 3rd
Thursday of each month

PODCAST

ENTRUSTED TO LEAD

With
Danita Cummins

Listen on
Apple Podcasts